HIDDEN BLOCK Quilts

- Discover New Blocks Inside Traditional Favorites

- 13 Quilt Settings • Instructions for 55 Blocks

Lerlene Nevaril

C&T PUBLISHING

© 2002 Lerlene Nevaril

Editor: Liz Aneloski
Technical Editor: Sara Kate MacFarland
Copyeditor: Stacy Chamness
Proofreader: Susan Nelsen
Cover Designer: Aliza Shalit
Design Director: Diane Pedersen
Book Designer: Dawn DeVries Sokol
Illustrator: Aliza Shalit
Production Assistant: Tim Manibusan
Photography: Jayne Nona Erickson, Sioux Falls, SD, unless otherwise noted
Published by C&T Publishing, Inc., P.O. Box 1456, Lafayette, California 94549

Front cover: *The Face in the Purple Vase*, 50" x 50", Lerlene Nevaril, quilted by Mary Roder of The Quiltworks
Back cover: *Carpenter's Wheel*, 49"x 49", Lerlene Nevaril, quilted by Mary Roder of The Quiltworks

Library of Congress Cataloging-in-Publication Data

Nevaril, Lerlene,
  Hidden block quilts : discover new blocks inside traditional favorites:
13 quilt settings, instructions for 55 blocks / Lerlene Nevaril.
      p. cm.
Includes bibliographical references.
  ISBN 1-57120-179-3
  1. Patchwork—Patterns. 2. Quilting—Patterns. I. Title.
  TT835 .N468 2002
  746.46'041—dc21
                              2002005117

Printed in China
10 9 8 7 6 5 4 3 2

CONTENTS

DEDICATION

To the memory of my maternal grandmother, Lerlene LeClair Holtzclaw Davis, who shared with me her name, as well as a love of sewing.

ACKNOWLEDGEMENTS

My thanks to Tomme Fent for challenging me to write the proposal for this book and for encouraging me at every step along the way. Thank you to Ann Brouillette, my partner at Heart & Hand Dry Goods, for giving me the time away from the shop to work on the book. Thanks for testing the block instructions go to Jan Gibson-Korytkowski, Tomme Fent, Susie Feathers, Joan Holloway, Jane Vereen, Pat Brenden, and Ginny Wing. Quilting turns patchwork into beautiful quilts, so thank you to Jan Gibson-Korytkowski, Mary Roder, Bonnie Lohry, and Boni Markve. Thank you to Jayne Erickson whose photography captured the quilting for all to see. Thank you to my editor, Liz Aneloski, and all at C&T who have encouraged me with their enthusiasm for this project. Thank you to my family members who have always believed I could do this.

PREFACE

Remember Hide and Seek, Treasure Hunt, and jigsaw puzzles? Maybe you've researched your family tree, explored space with a telescope, or enjoyed the wonder of planting bulbs and waiting to see what comes up in the spring. Whatever your personal choices, let's face it—we love the thrill of seeking out the unknown, of discovering something we've never seen before.

This book brings that search for the unknown into one of our favorite worlds—the world of quilting! Lerlene Nevaril takes us on a journey to find Hidden Blocks within block patterns we may have long since abandoned, becoming bored with the repetition of twelve blocks, side by side, with a border or two. She brings these traditional blocks back to life by showing us what's hidden inside them—like a package that keeps opening to reveal more and more surprises!

Come along with Lerlene to explore the Hidden Blocks she has found, and let her inspire you to find an infinite variety of new Hidden Blocks on your own. This design concept will open up a whole new world of quilts just waiting to be discovered!

Tomme J. Fent

INTRODUCTION

Several questions puzzled me in my early quilting days and I will pose them to you:

• How do you make a big quilt without having to repeat the same block over and over?
• What if the quilting stitch is not your strong point, so quilting every other plain block doesn't work for you?
• What if your block doesn't really blend well with one of the traditional alternate blocks?

One day the answer just popped up and things haven't been the same since. I was using the Arizona block to make a scrap quilt using some of the early Smithsonian reproduction fabrics (page 32). As I examined the block more closely, I saw that a nice design remained when I simply changed the outer row of colored triangles to the background color. This new "Hidden Block" gave the quilt a more open feeling than a standard setting of twenty-five of the same block placed in rows. The new block blended well with the original block because it was a variation.

As I looked, I began to find other blocks that could be used the same way. By changing the block a little, it could become the alternate block. Early Hidden Blocks were made by changing sections of the block to background fabric. Then, other possibilities of Hidden Blocks appeared. Where I shifted the location of elements of the original block, changed the coloration of some of the shapes, and changed some of the other shapes, more than one Hidden Block was made from the original.

As I continued to work with this design concept, I began to explore possibilities beyond just using the Hidden Blocks for alternate blocks. Suddenly, the first quilts I made began to look very primitive. I realized that Hidden Blocks could be clustered around the original block, and multiple blocks could be combined in multiple settings for added versatility. One idea or concept lead to another and another— and the end still is not in sight.

Hidden inside almost every quilt block is a whole quilt just waiting to be discovered.

HOW TO USE THIS BOOK

Someone once said that a picture is worth a thousand words, and this book is proof. It is long on illustration and short on text.

Chapters One and Two begin with the general techniques for bringing the blocks out of hiding. Chapter One explains the Hidden Block concept. It shows how to find Hidden Blocks by simply changing some of the colored patches to larger patches of background fabrics. Chapter Two shows how more changes can made by moving patches and changing their size and/or color. Chapter Three is a gallery of Hidden Block quilts. I recommend that you read the chapters in order for a better understanding of the technique. However, a quick peek at the Gallery of Quilts in Chapter Three (beginning on page 32) will show just how far you can take this concept.

Ten traditional blocks are presented. From two to seven options of Hidden Blocks are shown for each original block. Instructions are given for making fifty-seven Hidden Blocks. There is a short explanation of the techniques used to change the A Block into the B Blocks, C Blocks, etc. The number of settings shown for each block varies, with suggestions on color and fabric selection to help spark your creativity. When I worked up the designs, I tried as many as fifty or sixty different settings for some of the more complex blocks with multiple Hidden Blocks. This book can only present a small sampling, a starting point for your own quilts.

Each block is unique and requires a different approach to design. Reading a short description of how the Hidden Blocks were found for each original block and looking at the examples will train your eye to find other blocks. You will see that what works for one block may not work on the next. The examples illustrate the concepts and provide inspiration to ignite your thought processes.

Most of the quilt block patterns in this book are traditional. I used Barbara Brackman's *Encyclopedia of Pieced Quilt Patterns* as my primary source material. Many patterns will be readily recognizable. Others are not so well known. But when you alter these blocks, then mix all the versions together, you can get very pleasing designs. At first glance, some blocks may not seem to be good candidates for this process. Often these blocks become the biggest winners!

Chapter Four gives instructions for sample horizontal and on-point settings.

Chapter Five has instructions for making all of the blocks presented in Chapters One and Two, as well as cutting and fabric requirements for thirteen quilt settings in six block sizes. Chapter Six gives suggestions for spicing up the backs of your quilts.

Follow these guidelines to help you find Hidden Blocks and the quilts they make. Almost *any* quilt block can be given a new look. Change some of the colored patches to background fabric, change the size of some patches, or move them around in the block. The result will be a block that relates to and complements the original block. Quilts made from combinations of these blocks are interesting. The common patches flow easily from block to block, carrying a common theme throughout the quilt.

Become very familiar with graph paper and colored pencils, and/or a good computer quilt design program. Not all of the blocks you come up with will be winners, but the process will help educate your eye to see possibilities and probabilities. You will find yourself looking for Hidden Blocks in every block you see. Soon, all of your quilts will have a personality and uniqueness you have given them.

Armed with these instructions and ideas, you will be well on your way to designing one-of-a-kind quilts made with Hidden Blocks. Enjoy!

CHAPTER One

Bring the Blocks Out of Hiding

Quilters are always looking for new blocks and quilt designs. Sometimes all that is necessary to find new blocks is to look inside the traditional blocks—many of them contain hidden designs. Combining these new blocks with the traditional block can produce exciting new quilts.

You can use a computer quilt design program or draw the block on graph paper. Use tracing paper overlays and colored pencils to design and color Hidden Blocks on the graph paper. Take the time to draw out several of the setting layouts from Chapter Four and apply the blocks to them.

There are many ways to find Hidden Blocks. In blocks that have numerous divisions, the possibilities are almost endless. It becomes a question of what looks best—or how much openness you want in the new block. New blocks are created by changing the color and/or position of some patches. The possibilities can reach to infinity when patches change in design.

There is not just a single formula to find the Hidden Blocks; quilt blocks are very different, and their Hidden Blocks will be just as different. There are, however, some basic starting points. Begin with the first one and see what develops. If the first one doesn't work, go to the second, and on down the line, finding Hidden Blocks using one or several techniques.

1. The easiest Hidden Blocks to find appear simply by replacing the colored patches on the outside row with background fabric strips. When you place this new block next to the original, each block retains its own identity. You will get design separation without having to add sashing, as in the Arizona blocks below.

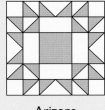 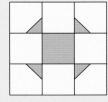

Arizona   Arizona Hidden Block

2. Instead of replacing the entire outer row, replace only some of the patches. You can replace the patches in the corners, or the patches in the middle of the row. On some blocks you can do both, and then you have two Hidden Blocks to mix with the original, as in the Fifty-four Forty or Fight and Weathervane blocks.

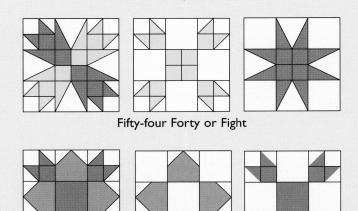

Fifty-four Forty or Fight

Weathervane

3. Many two-color-plus-background blocks offer easily designed Hidden Blocks. Patches of one color or the other can become interesting B and C Blocks. Sometimes both colors work, as in the Weathervane block.

In other cases, one color pattern works, but the second does not. In the Priscilla's Dream block, the blue squares form an X Block, but the pink triangles need the addition of color in the center square to stand alone as a separate block.

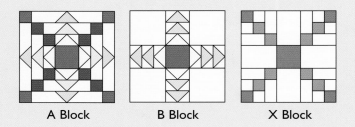

A Block   B Block   X Block

Sometimes Hidden Blocks can have "floating" patches of color. When viewed on their own they look strange, but it is their interaction with other blocks that makes an interesting quilt design.

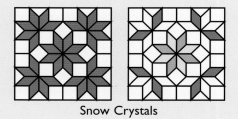

Snow Crystals

4. Look for designs within the block that can stand on their own. A good example of this is the Twist and Turn block. The B Block is a pinwheel shape design, and the C Block is a Monkey Wrench design.

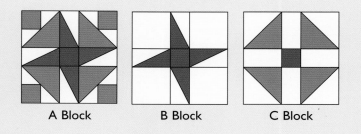

A Block   B Block   C Block

5. Most blocks with colored corner patches contain L and X Blocks. Priscilla's Dream is a good example. These blocks are very useful for framing other blocks within the body of the quilt.

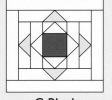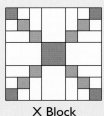

C Block   L Block   X Block

Another clue to finding L and X Blocks is the corner combination found in the Fifty-four Forty or Fight block. Although the corner square is background, the half-square triangles on each side of the corner square give the illusion of corner-to-corner color.

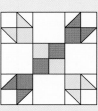

Fifty-four Forty or Fight

6. For blocks with many colored squares and rectangles, the number of Hidden Blocks is almost limitless. With blocks that have numerous divisions, begin replacing colored patches from the outside rows with background fabric and work your way to the center of the block. While you are replacing patches along the outside, see if you can create more Hidden Blocks by eliminating color in the interior of the block.

When looking for Hidden Blocks, try *everything*. Sometimes an idea is wrong for one block, but it may be just what the next one needs. This is a trial-and-error technique, but the results can be spectacular. The trial-and-error method of design is greatly enhanced by the use of a good computer quilt design program. This book would not have been possible without the EQ4 and Block Base programs from The Electric Quilt Company. In fifteen minutes, you can audition a block, recolor it, find one or more Hidden Blocks, and design several quilt layouts. Or you can come to the conclusion that there are no usable Hidden Blocks.

DEFINITION OF "ALPHABET" BLOCKS

When working with these blocks, I found A and B creeping into my notes. "A" always denotes the original block—the block with which you begin. The first alteration or modification of this block is the "B" Block. Thus, the next alteration becomes the "C" Block and so on.

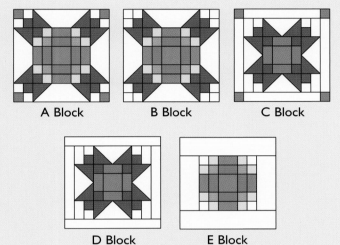

A Block   B Block   C Block

D Block   E Block

The exceptions are the L and X Blocks. In the L Block, colored patches form a single diagonal line across the block. These patches do not always have to be the same shape. They can include large and small squares, single triangles, or half-square triangle squares of color. It all depends on the patches in the original block.

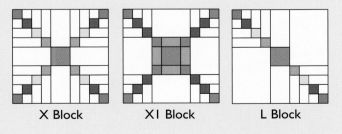

X Block   X1 Block   L Block

In the X Block, two diagonal lines form an X of color in the block. As with the L Block, the size and shape of the color patches can vary, and depend on the patches in the original block. The L and X Blocks are used like a lattice in the garden, a "form" on which to grow flowers. In a quilt, the lattice blocks provide a background to showcase the other blocks.

There are other blocks that act as lattice blocks that do not fit the L or X definition. In these blocks, there is an X formed, but the lines go from side to side. These blocks are not given a specific designation.

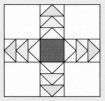

Priscilla's Dream

Carpenter's Wheel

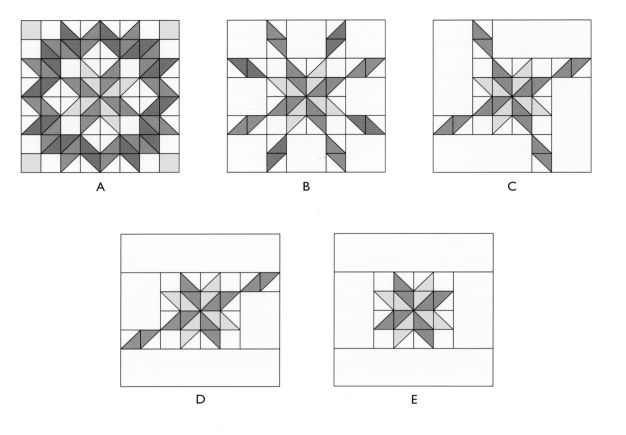

A

B

C

D

E

The Carpenter's Wheel was a very popular pieced pattern in the mid-1800s. This traditional quilt was made with or without sashing and often had dark backgrounds. This was not an easy pattern to piece. Each diamond shape had two off-grain sides and the background squares all had set-in seams. Redrafting the pattern to utilize half-square triangles instead of diamonds greatly simplifies construction of this block. Many of the bias edges and set-in seams are eliminated.

The B Block consists of the center star and one diamond at each of the star's points. The color of the outer points matches the color that was there on the A Block, so green diamonds are joined to the yellow points of the center star. Take care when piecing B Blocks so the position of the yellow and red diamonds in the center is reversed. This way, the outer points will match the color of the points they touch in the A Block.

The center star is repeated in the outer corners of the quilt. The C Block eliminates the green pieces, and the D Block, two opposite red pieces. These blocks have a lot of motion, which is clearly reflected in the quilts. Carpenter's Wheel 2 has plain borders to provide space for extraordinary quilting, or complementary appliqué.

Carpenter's Wheel 1

Carpenter's Wheel 2

Carpenter's Wheel 3

Carpenter's Wheel 4

Carpenter's Wheel 5

Carpenter's Wheel 6

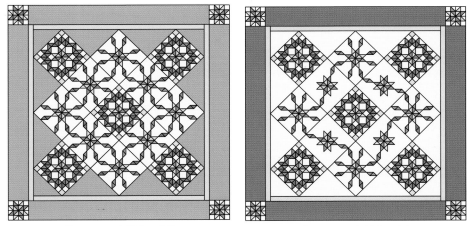

Carpenter's Wheel 7

Carpenter's Wheel 8

Carpenter's Wheel 9

Double Nine-Patch

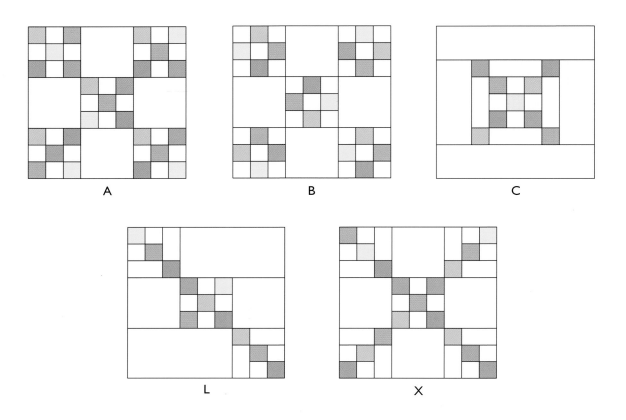

A

B

C

L

X

Even a block as simple as the Double Nine-Patch contains Hidden Blocks that can be used to make new and exciting quilts. Most of the quilts presented here use the A, L, and X Blocks. These designs are very open and romantic made up in soft pastels or '30s reproduction fabrics.

The B Block is made from four-color Nine-Patches and helps give the appearance of hearts in Quilt 9. The use of sashing with Nine-Patch corner squares gives a very open, airy look to Quilt 3.

These blocks are very versatile and look good in both horizontal and on-point settings.

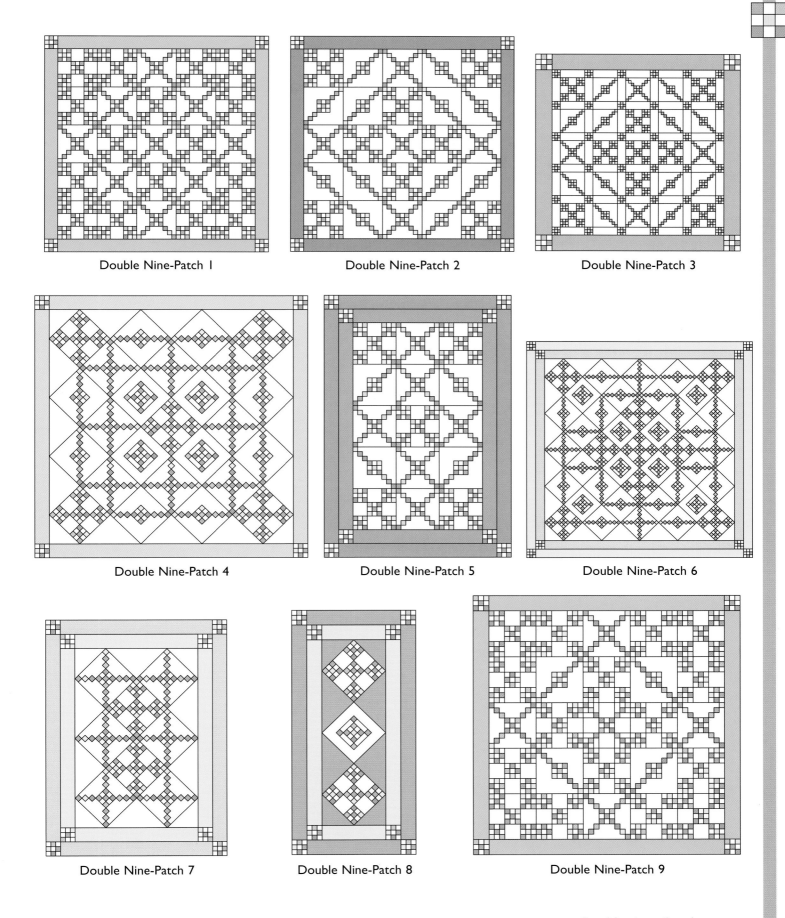

Double Nine-Patch 1

Double Nine-Patch 2

Double Nine-Patch 3

Double Nine-Patch 4

Double Nine-Patch 5

Double Nine-Patch 6

Double Nine-Patch 7

Double Nine-Patch 8

Double Nine-Patch 9

Fifty-four Forty or Fight

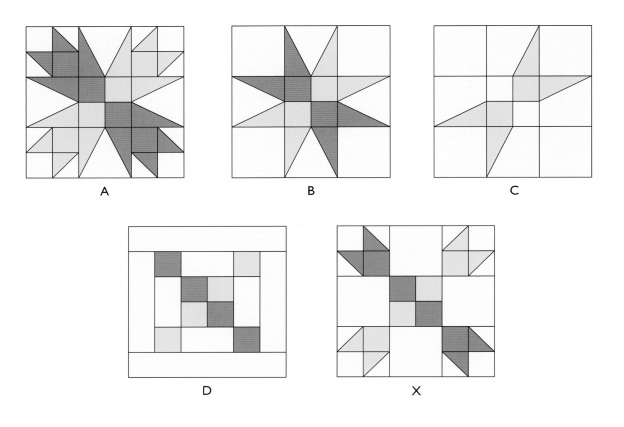

A

B

C

D

X

It's hard to say what the original block is for these quilts. The design lines of the block go by at least seven names, the most recognizable being Fifty-four Forty or Fight. On a basic level, the early quiltmakers were already discovering Hidden Blocks.

Fifty-four Forty or Fight 2 consists of the A and X Blocks. The "cactus blooms" of the A Block are the result of color placement. Repeat the same color pattern in the X Blocks. Adding sashing to match the background gives an openness that preserves the integrity of the individual blocks. When the Hidden Blocks differ from the A Block by only one or two patches, the extra separation of sashing often helps to define the individual design elements.

Borders in several of the quilts use the triangular design from the A Block. This gives motion to the border area of the quilt and relates back to the center of the quilt. These illustrate the versatility of the unit in border design. You can mix colors or use only one, and you can turn the unit in different directions for a variety of looks.

In Fifty-four Forty or Fight 4, 5, 7, 8, and 9, the C Blocks give the openness and movement usually provided by L Blocks. In Fifty-four Forty or Fight 7, the C Blocks form circles across the surface. This is a good place for appliqué and/or fancy quilting designs.

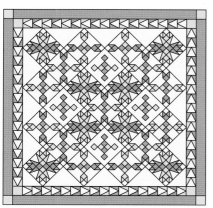

Fifty-four Forty or Fight 1

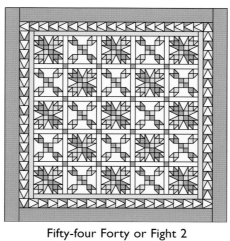

Fifty-four Forty or Fight 2

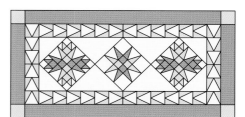

Fifty-four Forty or Fight 3

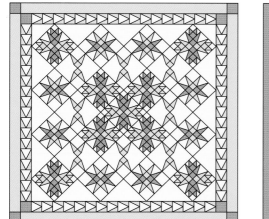

Fifty-four Forty or Fight 4

Fifty-four Forty or Fight 5

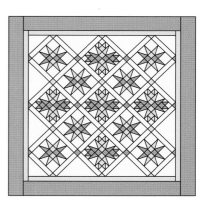

Fifty-four Forty or Fight 6

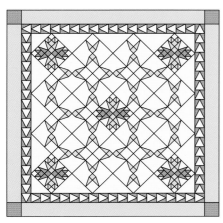

Fifty-four Forty or Fight 7

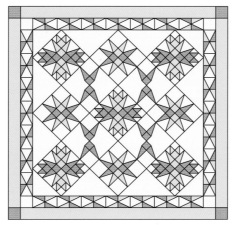

Fifty-four Forty or Fight 8

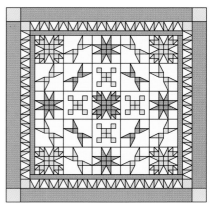

Fifty-four Forty or Fight 9

Hovering Hawks

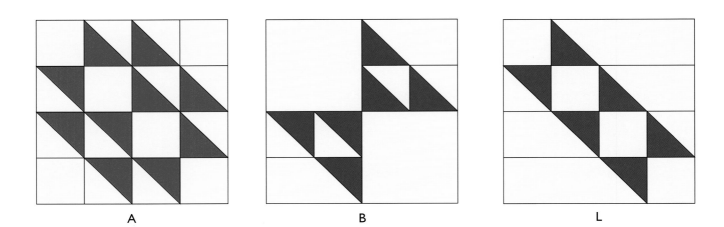

A   B   L

Hovering Hawks is a very simple block. The design ideas and Hidden Blocks come from simple color changes. No patches are moved or changed in any other way. There is no end to what you can imagine if you try. One idea leads to another, then another, and so on.

The L Block is hidden in the two center rows of triangles. The B Block merely leaves off the four triangles at the corners of the block. These blocks have a diagonal direction. Note that Hovering Hawks 2 is just Hovering Hawks 1 with the L Blocks rotated in the opposite direction. Notice how a red star is formed in Hovering Hawks 3 and 4 when the four A Blocks are pointed to the center. Look at the amount of motion created by changing the direction of the L Blocks in Hovering Hawks 4. Hovering Hawks 6 and 7 have the same blocks, but the direction is flipped.

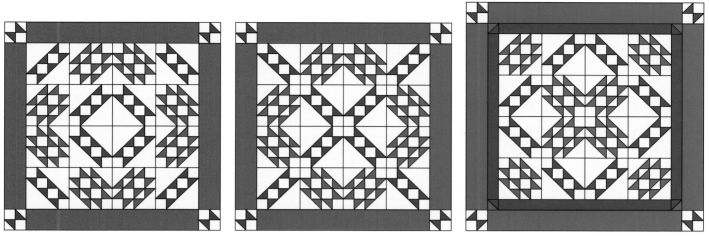

Hovering Hawks 1

Hovering Hawks 2

Hovering Hawks 3

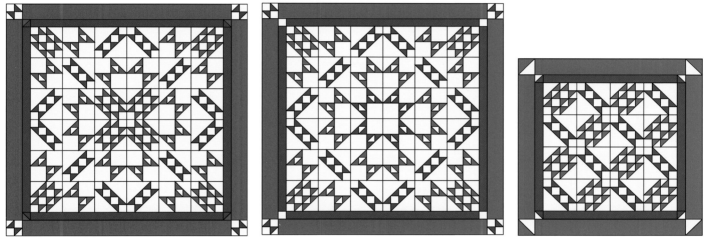

Hovering Hawks 4

Hovering Hawks 5

Hovering Hawks 6

Hovering Hawks 7

Hovering Hawks 8

Hovering Hawks 9

Priscilla's Dream

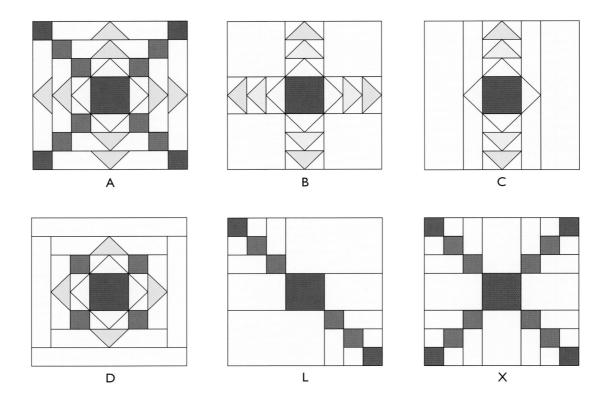

A   B   C

D   L   X

Five of the blocks hidden inside the Priscilla's Dream block are presented here. There are probably more blocks, but this is enough to keep you designing for hours. The telescoping nature of the A Block contains Hidden Blocks that scale down in size, giving rise to some very sophisticated designs.

The B and X Blocks are the real stars in these examples. They add dazzle and movement to the quilts. When either of these blocks is placed next to the A Block, the lines of squares or triangles are continuous and have great impact on the design, as in Priscilla's Dream 5–9. In Priscilla's Dream 4, the color of the setting triangles is the same as the outer border. This makes the dark inner border appear to float on top of a single, light, outer border.

Priscilla's Dream 1

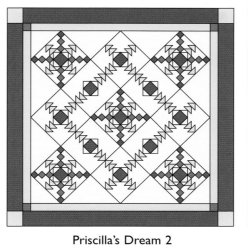

Priscilla's Dream 2

Priscilla's Dream 3

Priscilla's Dream 4

Priscilla's Dream 5

Priscilla's Dream 6

Priscilla's Dream 7

Priscilla's Dream 8

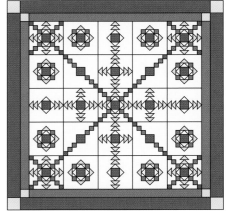

Priscilla's Dream 9

CHAPTER Two

More Ways to Bring the Blocks Out of Hiding

Chapter One described six techniques for discovering Hidden Blocks. The techniques in this chapter, dealing with moving or changing shapes and color, are not as easy to categorize. These techniques are more specifically geared to the configuration of the A Block. As well as giving specific steps to follow, they also open your mind to see the possibilities hiding in individual blocks.

1. Remove an inner row and move the outside row in, replacing the outside row with background strips. Depending on the original block, this can work in different ways. This technique is used to design the B Block for the Bear's Paw block. The B Block deletes the second row in, and uses only eight of the half-square triangle patches from the outside row. The C Block adds more color to the center nine patch of the B Block.

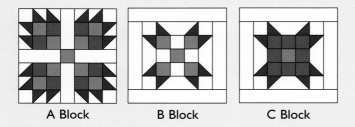

| A Block | B Block | C Block |

The Game Cocks D Block eliminates a row next to the block's center and moves the outer rows in. In order to make them fit, the square between the half-square triangles in the outer row is also eliminated. The new D Block retains many design lines of the A Block.

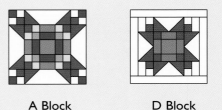

A Block　　　　D Block

2. In the Arrowhead block, changing the length of the "arrowheads" results in the E Block. The D Block changes the arrowhead to a square on point. These blocks retain a strong relationship to the A Block and provide many design opportunities. As long as the Hidden Blocks retain the feel of the A Block, changes can take many forms.

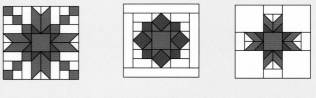

A Block　　　　D Block　　　　E Block

3. In addition to changing the color of individual patches within a block, you can find new design possibilities by changing the background color of blocks, as in the *Northwoods Winter* quilt (page 21).

Northwoods Winter
2000, 84" x 84"
Lerlene Nevaril, quilted by Mary Roder of
The Quiltworks

I used the Arizona block (page 7) to make a
Moda trunk show quilt. Using two background fabrics
adds a secondary design to the quilt.

Arrowhead

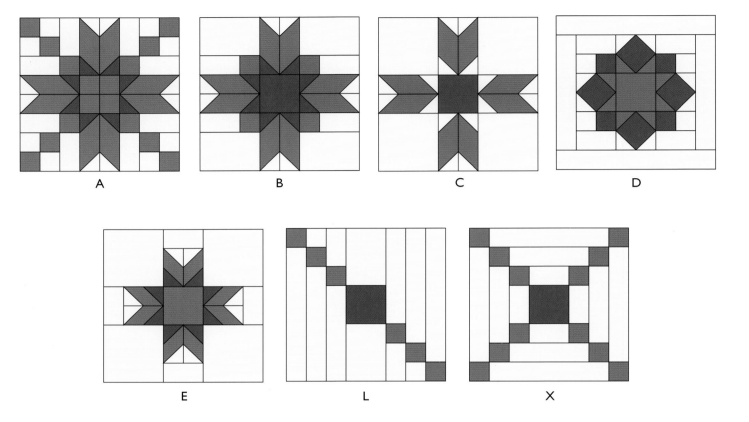

A   B   C   D

E   L   X

There are both star and lattice Hidden Blocks in the Arrowhead block. The L and X Blocks are taken from the large and small squares in the A Block. As with other blocks, combining these two blocks produces an open lattice effect. This effect can be seen by comparing Quilts 2, 6, 7, and 9.

The B and C Blocks are designed by taking away the small squares and recoloring the center square. A star is formed by color placement in the center of the B Block. In the E Block the original arrowhead shapes are shortened and the result is a star-in-a-star design. The D Block is an example of changing shapes to come up with a new, but coordinated, block. The long arrows in the center sides were changed to squares on-

point. The color of the innermost small squares was changed to match the other squares in the D Block. This gives the block a medallion look, and brings out the star that is formed around the center square. Done in red and green, the design would have a definite holiday look. Done in blue and white snowflake fabrics, it would have a wintry look. Use the blue for the background area and the white for the colored patches.

In Arrowhead 1 and 3, the small squares in the A Blocks connect with the squares in the L Blocks to form a frame around the center blocks. The L and X Blocks in Arrowhead 2 form a double lattice. In the *Midsummer Madness* quilt on page 35, this space is filled with feather quilting.

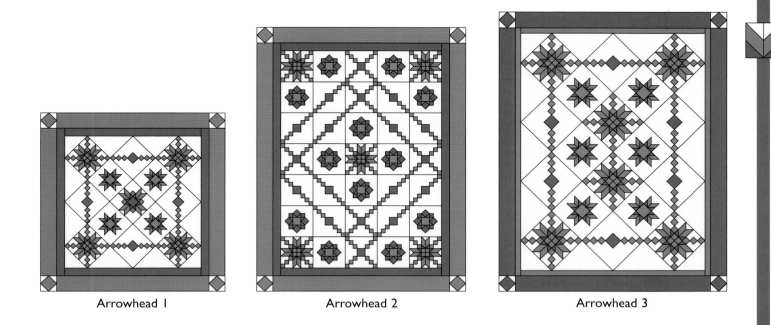

Arrowhead 1   Arrowhead 2   Arrowhead 3

Arrowhead 4   Arrowhead 5   Arrowhead 6

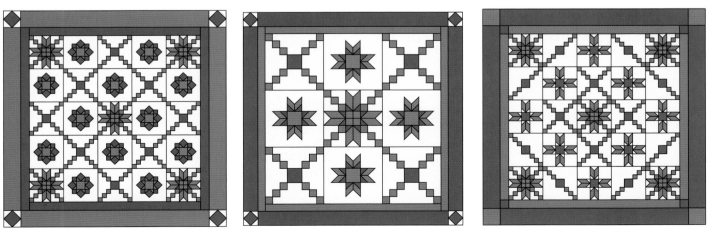

Arrowhead 7   Arrowhead 8   Arrowhead 9

Bear's Paw

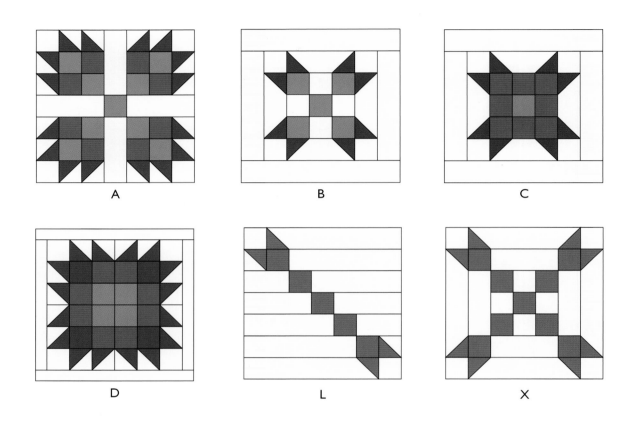

A   B   C

D   L   X

The Bear's Paw block is a very simple design. It consists of four "paws" rotated around a small square. It doesn't contain many Hidden Blocks, so it is surprising how many quilts it can generate.

The five colored squares in the center of the B Block are identical to those in the A Block. The half-square triangles can be found at the tips of the bear's paws. In this case, color wasn't simply changed to background, but the half-square triangles were moved toward the center of the block. This shape block appears in many Hidden Blocks. In fact, this block pops up so often it should be added to any list of alternate blocks.

Color is added to the side squares in the center of the B Block to form a very different-looking C Block. The X Block is formed by leaving all

of the diagonal patches of the A Block in place and coloring them the same. The L Block is formed from the X Block.

All of the blocks look good in either horizontal or on-point settings. Use autumn colors to make very graphic, country quilts.

Bear's Paw 1 was the first quilt in the series, and uses only A and B Blocks. (See Photo on page 32 in Chapter Three.) Bear's Paw 2 and 3 show the extra interest generated by using several Hidden Blocks with the A Block. In Bear's Paw 2, using the same color for the setting triangles and outer border makes the design area seem to float. Bear's Paw 5 uses three Hidden Blocks, but not the A Block. It is a much lighter-looking quilt.

Bear's Paw 1

Bear's Paw 2

Bear's Paw 3

Bear's Paw 4

Bear's Paw 5

Bear's Paw 6

Bear's Paw 7

Bear's Paw 8

Bear's Paw 9

Bear's Paw   25

Diamond Star

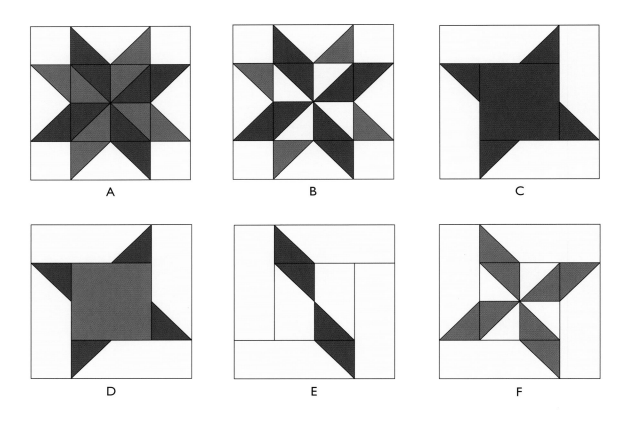

A

B

C

D

E

F

Diamond Star is a four-patch block and does not offer many possibilities for Hidden Blocks. However, the Hidden Blocks that do exist are very dynamic and have a lot of motion. The resulting quilts are simple but different. The quilt *Diamond Stars — Wild and Crazy*, on page 34, is composed of only two blocks, but the use of many bright fabrics makes it pop.

Though these blocks are all very similar, they form interesting patterns when combined in quilts. Blocks C and D have the openness of E and F Blocks, but do not give a lattice effect. In Diamond Star 3, 4, and 5, the E and F blocks provide a more ribbon-like effect. These blocks are very effective in both horizontal and on-point settings.

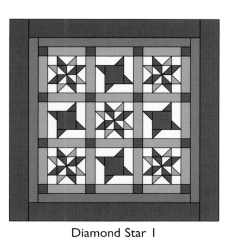

Diamond Star 1

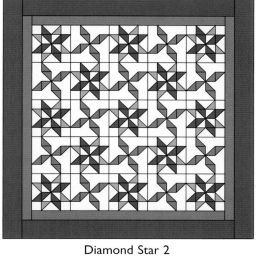

Diamond Star 2

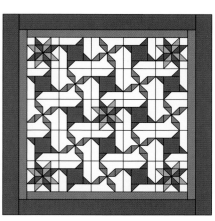

Diamond Star 3

Diamond Star 4

Diamond Star 5

Diamond Star 6

Diamond Star 7

Diamond Star 8

Diamond Star 9

Game Cocks

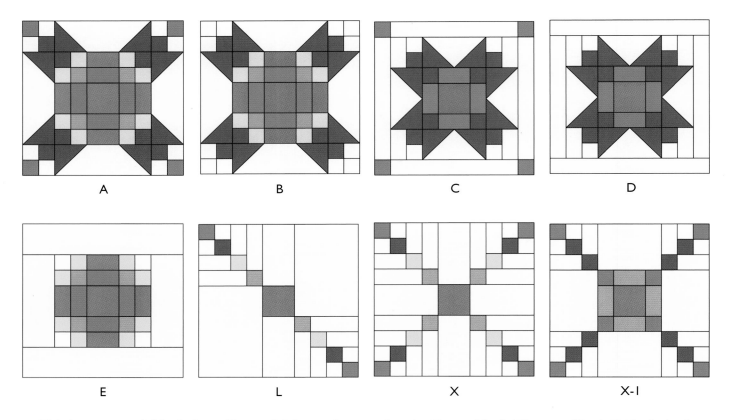

A　　　　　B　　　　　C　　　　　D

E　　　　　L　　　　　X　　　　　X-1

This is a ten-patch block that offers multiple possibilities for Hidden Blocks. The B Block simply removes the small, green outer corner squares. The C Block puts these small squares back in, but takes out an interior row (red rectangles and yellow squares) and moves the remaining color toward the center. The D Block begins with the C Block and takes out the corner squares again. These squares can cause distracting, or attractive, spots of color where several blocks come together.

The E Block takes away the outer two rows of patches and a small dark blue square. Leaving out the small blue squares from the corners makes this block appear to have a rounded shape. The combination of the various block shapes makes interesting settings in either horizontal or on-point settings. The L and X Blocks have a smaller center square. The X-1 Block adds a second round of color in the center, forming a

heavier X-type block. The use of both X Blocks in the same quilt is a great design advantage.

Game Cocks 4 is an example of the medallion effect achieved by grouping four of the same block together. Place these four blocks off-center and surround them with X, X-1, and L Blocks for more of an art quilt look. Game Cocks 4, 7, and 9 show the many variations available by combining the L, X, and X-1 Blocks.

Imagine the many settings made possible by substituting and rearranging the A through E Blocks. Game Cocks 6 illustrates one of the advantages of using the C Block with the corner squares. These corner squares, in combination with sashing and corner posts, give the illusion of Nine-Patch blocks surrounding the center block.

Game Cocks 8 looks much more open than the similar Game Cocks 7 because of the use of sashing that matches the background. Substituting L Blocks for X Blocks also adds to the more open feeling.

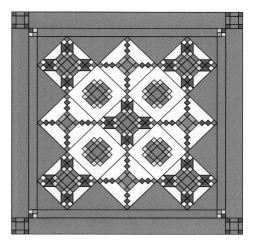

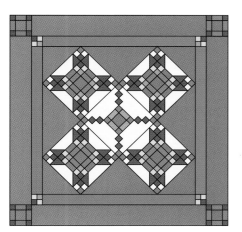

Game Cocks 1

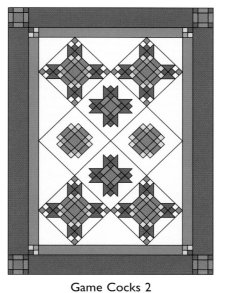

Game Cocks 2

Game Cocks 3

Game Cocks 4

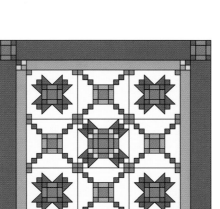

Game Cocks 5

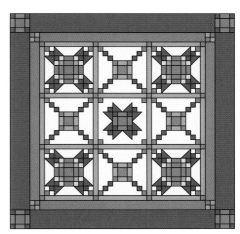

Game Cocks 6

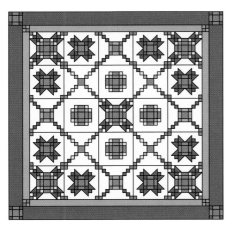

Game Cocks 7

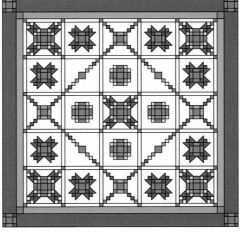

Game Cocks 8

Game Cocks 9

Weathervane

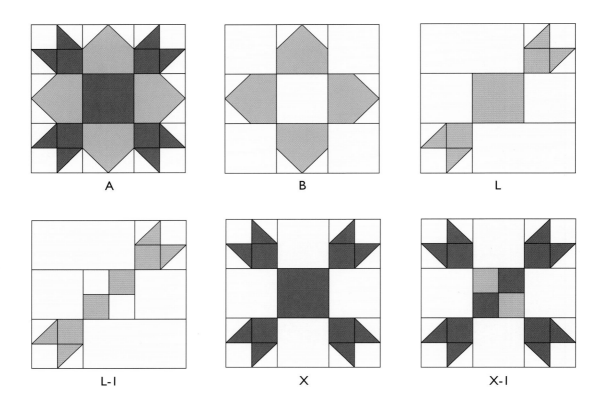

A

B

L

L-1

X

X-1

This block, on its own, has two different looks which depend on the placement of light and dark fabrics. Dark colors leap out and become the prominent shapes in the block. Hidden Blocks can be made using either the mid-size five-sided squares (B Block) or the center and corner units (X Block).

Use of a single print or floral in the B Block creates a coordinated quilt. The X Block looks good whether you use a single fabric for all blocks in a quilt or a different fabric for each. Plain, marble, or tone-on-tone fabrics work best because there are two triangles and a square of color in each corner unit. The L-1 and X-1 Blocks are formed by turning the large center square into a Four-Patch. Notice the difference they make between Weathervane 4 and 5, and 6 and 8.

Weathervane 1

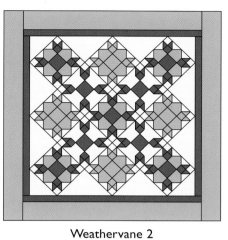

Weathervane 2

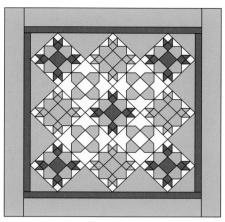

Weathervane 3

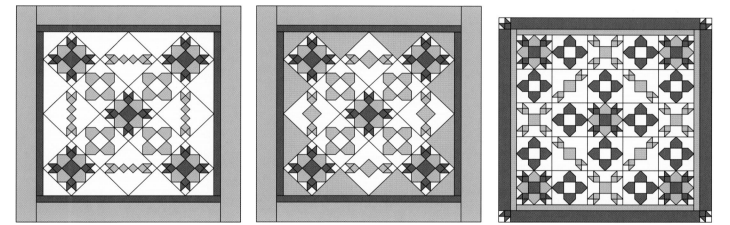

Weathervane 4

Weathervane 5

Weathervane 6

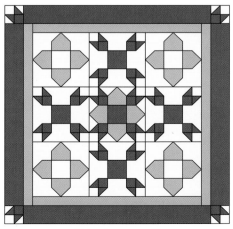

Weathervane 7

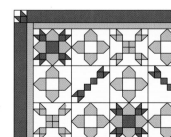

Weathervane 8

CHAPTER Three

Gallery of Quilts

And Just a Little Less
1996, 80" x 80"
Lerlene Nevaril, quilted by
Sgt. Bluff Methodist
Quilters

This is the quilt that started
it all. Fabrics are from the
first Smithsonian reproduction collections. The quilt
uses the Arizona block
(page 7).

Indian Puzzle
1997, 72" x 72"
Lerlene Nevaril, quilted by
Sgt. Bluff Methodist
Quilters

This is the second quilt.
It is also made with
reproduction fabrics.

Expressions of Nature ▲
1999, 70" x 70"
Lerlene Nevaril, quilted by
Boni Markve of Threads
That Bind

This Bear's Paw quilt was
designed for Moda's "Second
Nature" trunk show. The
dark setting triangles help
focus attention on the blocks
in the center.

Holiday Magic Mystery
2001, 55" x 55"
Lerlene Nevaril,
Mary Roder of
The Quiltworks

This Bear's Paw was designed as a mystery class. While auditioning fabrics for the setting triangles, I decided to use two fabrics. This look may not be for everyone, but it does seem to draw you into the quilt.

Two Weathervanes
1999, 64" x 64"
Lerlene Nevaril, quilted by Boni Markve of
Threads That Bind

Two Weathervanes was made with the same Moda fabrics as *Expressions of Nature* (page 32), this time in flannel.

Candy Vanes
2001, 47" x 47"
Lerlene Nevaril, quilted by Mary Roder of The Quiltworks

Candy Vanes, a second Weathervane block quilt, is the result of a strip-piecing class with Shelly Burge. The bright fabrics and L blocks give this quilt a playful feeling.

Off-Center—Out of Control
2000, 44" x 51"
Lerlene Nevaril, quilted by Bonnie Lohry of Valley Quilting

This version of the Hovering Hawks block is a real toss-up of color and design. This was made as a result of a challenge to use different color families on either side of the blocks' diagonal line.

Diamond Stars— Wild and Crazy
2000, 42" x 42"
Lerlene Nevaril, quilted by Bonnie Lohry of Valley Quilting

Black is a good background choice for showcasing bright colors to the best advantage. Random use of many different fabrics gives a vibrancy to the sashing and borders.

Carpenter's Wheel
2001, 49" x 49"
Lerlene Nevaril, quilted by Mary Roder of The Quiltworks

This updated version of a nineteenth century pattern gets much of its charm from the reproduction fabrics. The yellow corner squares help to visually connect the main blocks.

Small Christmas Star
2000, 50" x 50"
Lerlene Nevaril, quilted by Lerlene and by Bonnie Lohry of Valley Quilting

This Arrowhead block quilt is another challenge quilt: Use a focus fabric in the center square of a split Nine-Patch block.

Midsummer Madness
2001, 76" x 100"
Lerlene Nevaril, quilted by Mary Roder of The Quiltworks

This is another mystery quilt. The L and X Blocks form a lattice, or frame, for the wonderful feather wreath quilting.

Black & White and Red All Over
2001, 44" x 44"
Lerlene Nevaril, quilted by Bonnie Lohry of Valley Quilting

In this version the Arrowhead block is turned on point. It relies on the L Blocks and color formula for its dynamic impact.

Desert Rose
2001, 60" x 60"
Lerlene Nevaril, quilted by
Jan Gibson-Korytkowski of
Quilting Memories & More

This Priscilla's Dream quilt
gets its name from the
coral, sand, and turquoise
fabrics used and from prim-
roses in the quilting.

July Celebrations
2001, 42" x 42"
Lerlene Nevaril, quilted by Bonnie Lohry of Valley
Quilting

This Game Cocks variation uses many red, blue,
and gold fabrics in a small patriotic wallhanging.

Harlequin Lights
2001, 100" x 100"
Lerlene Nevaril, quilted by Jan Gibson-
Korytkowski of Quilting Memories & More

Oversized Game Cocks blocks make this a king-
size quilt. I was experimenting with an asymmet-
rical layout. The bright colors of the fabrics and
the variegated quilting thread suggested the name
for this quilt.

Christmas Cactus
2000, 66" x 66"
Lerlene Nevaril, quilted by Bonnie Lohry of Valley Quilting

This quilt uses the Fifty-four Forty or Fight block. The sashing helps to isolate the blocks so they retain their identity.

Cactus Table Runner
2001, 22" x 46"
Lerlene Nevaril, quilted by Bonnie Lohry of Valley Quilting

Multiple fabrics and two different blocks give even this small table runner interest and excitement.

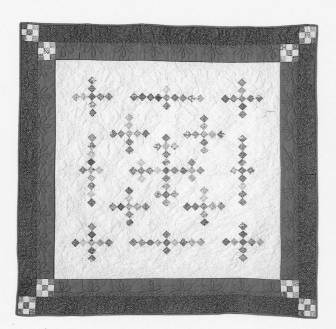

Lullabye Patches
2002, 50" x 50"
Lerlene Nevaril, quilted by Mary Roder of The Quiltworks

Thirties reproduction fabrics team with the Double Nine-Patch block to make a soft quilt for a special baby.

Pinwheel Stars
2002, 54" x 54"
Lerlene Nevaril,
quilted by Mary
Roder of The
Quiltworks

The use of three
Hidden Blocks and
multiple color choices
brings a great sense of
movement to this quilt.

**The Face in the
Purple Vase**
2002, 50" x 50"
Lerlene Nevaril,
quilted by Mary Roder
of The Quiltworks

The vases in the block
centers are reflected
in the very large quilt-
ed vase in the center
of the quilt. Block cen-
ters, as in these
Weathervane blocks,
are a great place to
showcase specialty
fabrics.

Folk Art Wedding Vanes
2000, 60" x 60"
Lerlene Nevaril, quilted by
Bonnie Lohry of Valley Quilting

Here is another Weathervane
block quilt. The pattern is the
same as *Two Weathervanes*, but
the pastel fabrics give it a very
soft, feminine look.

Toile of the Day
2001, 45" x 45"
Lerlene Nevaril, quilted by Mary
Roder of The Quiltworks

The many colors of blue in the toile
offered opportunity to pull in several
blue fabrics. Contrast this soft
Diamond Star block quilt with
Diamond Stars—Wild and Crazy.

CHAPTER
four

Quilt Settings

GENERAL DESIGN GUIDELINES

Setting possibilities are almost endless with Hidden Block quilts. If you are working only with A and B Blocks there is a finite number of combinations and settings. When you start working with three or more blocks, the numbers jump. The number of possible combinations changes with each set of blocks. A setting that works for one set of blocks may not work for the next. The designs of the different blocks often dictate particular settings to use. Some blocks look better in horizontal settings; others, on-point. There are few rules. It is a trial and error approach. Suitability is unpredictable and adds surprise to the process.

The settings presented here are just a suggestion and starting point. Most of the settings combine the A Block with one or more

other blocks. Some of the very complex A Blocks produce many simpler Hidden Blocks. You may even want to leave out a heavy A Block if you want a quilt with a lighter feel.

You should consider the settings presented in this chapter as a simple framework. They help you get started.

Most often you will begin with the A Block. Its placement distributes weight within the setting. If you are using settings with L and X Blocks, they should be put in place next. Their directional properties often dictate their placement. Using the L Blocks can introduce a sense of openness to the setting. After the A, L, and X Blocks are in place, audition B, C, D and so on Blocks to fill in. You will find that all blocks do not work in all settings. The examples below illustrate some possible starting settings.

Use of sashings and corner squares is subjective and depends on the blocks used. Using the background fabric as sashing can open up a quilt with complex blocks. Colored sashing can be used to frame and separate blocks and give them importance.

There are two general types of settings presented here: horizontal and on-point. In the horizontal setting, the blocks are square to the sides of the quilt. In the on-point settings, blocks are turned diagonally. Study the examples to find the ones that appeal to you most. These will be your starting point. There are thousands of quilts just waiting to be created with the blocks and fabrics you like.

Horizontal Settings

This 1 block x 3 block (1 x 3) setting is the most basic. You can use any combination of blocks in this setting. Most blocks will work in this setting, but the L Block is too directional to be used. This is a good setting for table runners or for a tall, skinny wall space that needs a quilt.

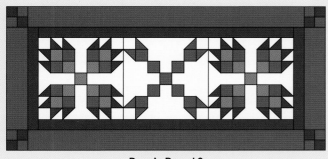

Bear's Paw 10

Double Nine-Patch 10 illustrates the 3 x 3 setting. This setting is a very popular for wall quilts, table toppers, and baby quilts. In this quilt, sashing extends the blocks and makes the quilt look more open. The repeat of the Nine-Patch in the corner squares and the border helps tie the design together.

Priscilla's Dream 6 is a 3 x 5 setting. The X

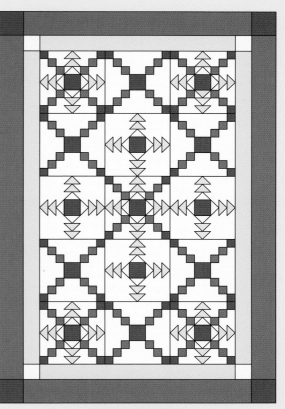

Priscilla's Dream 6

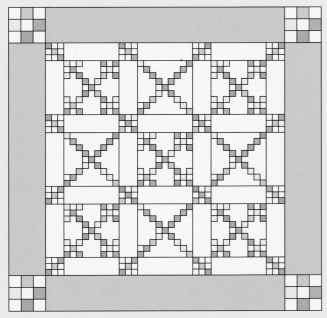

Double Nine-Patch 10

Blocks form an overall diagonal grid.

We are constantly told that groups of odd numbers are more interesting than groups of even numbers; but look at the movement provided in Hovering Hawks 2, a 4 x 4 setting. The design of both A and B Blocks is diagonal in nature, and provides a lot of motion.

The 5 x 5 setting is very useful. There are center points on each side with an equal number of blocks on each side. This feature offers possibilities for simple alter-

Hovering Hawks 2

nate settings, as in Diamond Star 10. Most sets of blocks have complex, or heavy blocks combined with simple, or light blocks. Try moving these blocks around to give the quilts totally different looks. Do you want it light in the center, and heavy around the outside, or just the opposite? Or do you want to alternate light and heavy blocks for a more balanced look? Even more possibilities pop up when you change block colors. In Bear's Paw 11 one set of blocks is replaced by a second row of L Blocks. This forms overlapping rectangles, and opens up the design even more.

The final set of horizontal settings is 5 x 7. These settings really illustrate L and X Block design possibilities. The diamond and rectangle configurations give many of these quilts the look of oriental carpets or tile floors. Use them to add new interest to your larger quilts.

Game Cocks 10

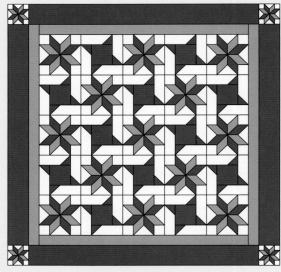

Diamond Star 10

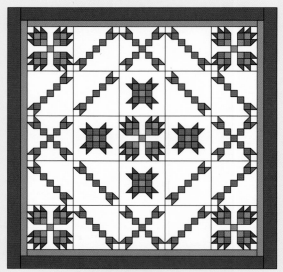

Bear's Paw 11

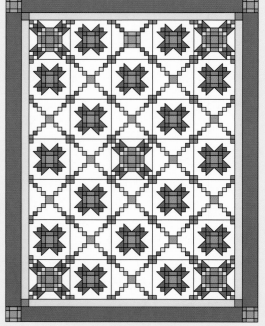

Game Cocks 11

ON-POINT SETTINGS

Fifty-four Forty or Fight 3 illustrates the 1 x 3 setting. As in the horizontal setting of the same size, any blocks may be used. If you are making a vertical wall-hanging, you can use three different blocks, beginning with the lightest, at the top, moving to the heaviest at the bottom. A configuration like the one shown is also suitable for use as a table runner.

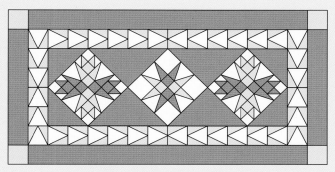

Fifty-four Forty or Fight 3

The 2 x 3 setting is very versatile for small quilts. In Bear's Paw 12 the same block is used in the top and bottom rows. The center four blocks are two different blocks. but they could all be the same block.

Bear's Paw 12

Game Cocks 12 and Double Nine-Patch 11 illustrate how L and X Blocks can be used in this setting, alone or in combination.

Game Cocks 12

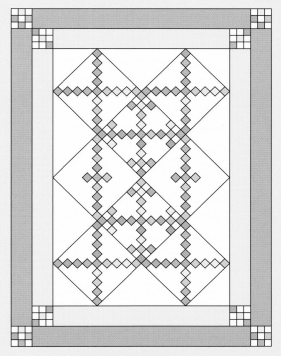

Double Nine-Patch 11

Quilt Settings   43

Diamond Star 11 is a 2 x 4 setting. This setting tends to be long and narrow, but it offers some interesting possibilities for multiple-block layouts.

Arrowhead 10 is a 3 x 4 setting. The L Blocks form a frame around the center blocks.

Arrowhead 10

Diamond Star 11

The 3 x 3 setting is popular and very versatile. Bear's Paw 13 illustrates a simple two-block configuration.

Diamond Star 8 is a 4 x 4 setting. This setting is well-suited for rows of blocks which radiate out from the center.

Bear's Paw 13

Diamond Star 8

Fifty-four Forty or Fight 7

Bear's Paw 14 and Game Cocks 13 are both 5 x 5 designs. The 5 x 5 on-point setting has 41 blocks (as opposed to 25 in the horizontal setting). These settings benefit from the liberal use of L and X Blocks. Assymetrical, modern settings can also be achieved.

Fifty-four Forty or Fight 7 illustrates one possible setting using only two blocks. The blank spaces offer excellent opportunities for appliqué or trapunto.

Bear's Paw 14

Double Nine-Patch 12

Double Nine-Patch 12 is a 4 x 5 setting. This large setting offers unlimited possibilities for designs using L and/or X Blocks.

Game Cocks 13

CHAPTER Five

Construction Guidelines

This chapter gives instructions for making the traditional and Hidden Blocks shown in Chapters One and Two. It also provides fabric requirements and cutting instructions for thirteen horizontal and on-point settings using the six block sizes included. Following are some basic instructions to use as you make your blocks and quilts.

Sew and Flip Technique: This is a technique for making triangles using only squares and rectangles. Two fabrics are placed right sides together. Sew along the marked diagonal. Trim and flip the top fabric, and press. The first fabric must be trimmed before a second is placed on top of it. Refer to the diagrams for reference as you work.

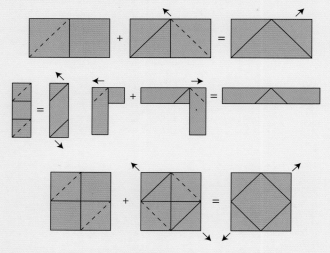

Half-square Triangles: These units are made from the 2⅜", 2⅞", and 3⅞" squares listed in the block instructions. Place two squares right sides together. Mark the diagonal line on the lighter fabric and sew ¼" on each side of the marked line. Cut on the diagonal line and press toward the darker piece.

Half-square triangles can also be made using Triangles

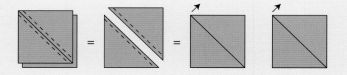

on a Roll or Thangles papers which can be purchased (page 93). Using the papers can often produce a more accurate pieced unit. If using the papers, you can increase the accuracy by pressing the units open before removing the papers. The papers stabilize the bias seam and help to prevent stretching out of shape.

Triangle Units: The Fifty-four Forty or Fight blocks have isosceles triangle units that require templates. Trace pattern provided to make your own templates, or use one of the available commercial templates: Tri-Recs Tools by EZ, or Perfect Patchwork Templates Set C by Marti Michell.

Cutting and Piecing Quilt Borders: Cutting measurements for quilt borders are exact and include ¼" seam allowances. It is always important to measure your quilt top and cut the borders accordingly, since the actual border lengths you need may be longer or shorter than listed. If you want to cut the borders before the top is finished, add two to three inches to the lengths listed. It is better to have to trim off rather than to add on. If it becomes necessary to piece the border strip, use diagonal seams. The piecing will be less noticeable in a print, and is a more pleasing join.

Side Triangles for On-Point Settings: Side triangles are sized slightly larger than needed to allow for individual piecing variances. Once all the rows are sewn together, trim the outside edges to allow ¼" seam allowances at block points.

Backing: Yardage is based on piecing the backing with vertical seams.

Arrowhead Block

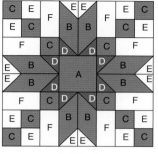

A Block

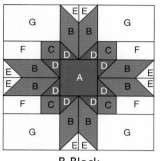

B Block

Finished Size	Color	Piece	Cut	Size
8" 1" unit		A	1	2½" x 2½"
		B	8	1½" x 3½"
		C	12	1½" x 1½"
		D	8	1½" x 1½"
		E	16	1½" x 1½"
		F	8	1½" x 2½"
12" 1½" unit		A	1	3½" x 3½"
		B	8	2" x 5"
		C	12	2" x 2"
		D	8	2" x 2"
		E	16	2" x 2"
		F	8	2" x 3½"

Finished Size	Color	Piece	Cut	Size
8" 1" unit		C	4	1½" x 1½"
		B	8	1½" x 3½"
		A	1	2½" x 2½"
		D	8	1½" x 1½"
		E	8	1½" x 1½"
		F	4	1½" x 2½"
		G	4	2½" x 3½"
12" 1½" unit		C	4	2" x 2"
		B	8	2" x 5"
		A	1	3½" x 3½"
		D	8	2" x 2"
		E	8	2" x 2"
		F	4	2" x 3½"
		G	4	3½" x 5"

STEP 1

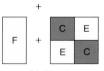

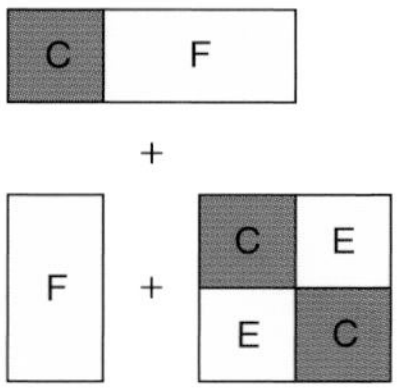

Make 4.

STEP 2

Make 4. Make 4 reversed.

STEP 3

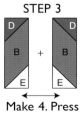

Make 4. Press seam open.

STEP 4

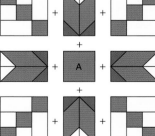

STEP 1

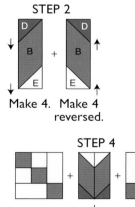

Make 4.

STEP 2

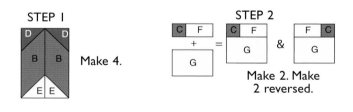

Make 2. Make 2 reversed.

STEP 3

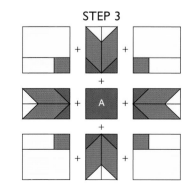

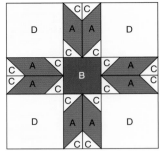

Arrowhead Block

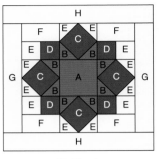

C Block

D Block

Finished Size	Color	Piece	Cut	Size
8" 1" Unit		A	8	1½" x 3½"
		B	1	2½" x 2½"
		C	16	1½" x 1½"
		D	4	3½" x 3½"
12" 1½" unit		A	8	2" x 5"
		B	1	3½" x 3½"
		C	16	2" x 2"
		D	4	5" x 5"

Finished Size	Color	Piece	Cut	Size
8" 1" unit		A	1	2½" x 2½"
		B	8	1½" x 1½"
		C	4	2½" x 2½"
		D	4	1½" x 1½"
		E	12	1½" x 1½"
		F	4	1½" x 2½"
		G	2	1½" x 6½"
		H	2	1½" x 8½"
12" 1½" unit		A	1	3½" x 3½"
		B	8	2" x 2"
		C	4	3½" x 3½"
		D	4	2" x 2"
		E	12	2" x 2"
		F	4	2" x 3½"
		G	2	2" x 9½"
		H	2	2" x 12½"

STEP 1

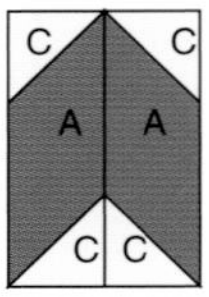

Make 4. Press
seams open.

STEP 1

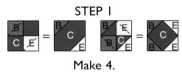

Make 4.

STEP 2

E + D = E D
+
F
= E D & D E
   F   F

Make 2. Make
2 reversed.

STEP 2

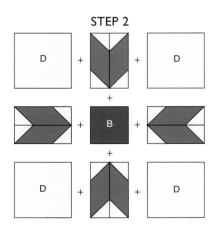

STEP 3

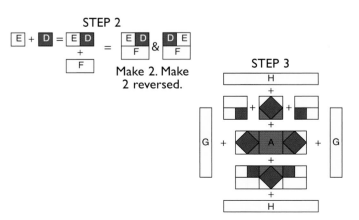

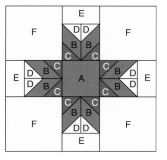

E Block

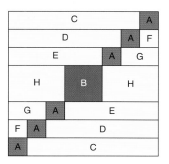

L Block

Finished Size	Color	Piece	Cut	Size
8"		A	1	2½" x 2½"
1" unit		B	8	1½" x 2½"
		C	8	1½" x 1½"
		D	8	1½" x 1½"
		E	4	1½" x 2½"
		F	4	3½" x 3½"
12"		A	1	3½" x 3½"
1½" unit		B	8	2" x 3½"
		C	8	2" x 2"
		D	8	2" x 2"
		E	4	2" x 3½"
		F	4	5" x 5"

Finished Size	Color	Piece	Cut	Size
8"		A	6	1½" x 1½"
1" unit		B	1	2½" x 2½"
		C	2	1½" x 7½"
		D	2	1½" x 6½"
		E	2	1½" x 5½"
		F	2	1½" x 1½"
		G	2	1½" x 2½"
		H	2	2½" x 3½"
12"		A	6	2" x 2"
1½" unit		B	1	3½" x 3½"
		C	2	2" x 11"
		D	2	2" x 9½"
		E	2	2" x 8"
		F	2	2" x 2"
		G	2	2" x 3½"
		H	2	3½" x 5"

STEP 1

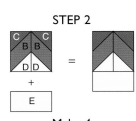

Make 4.

STEP 2

Make 4.

STEP 3

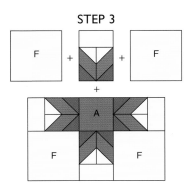

STEP 1

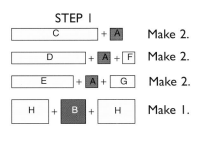

C + A   Make 2.

D + A + F   Make 2.

E + A + G   Make 2.

H + B + H   Make 1.

STEP 2

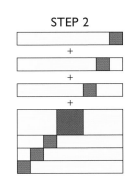

Arrowhead Block

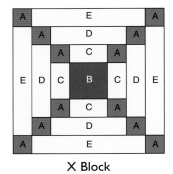

X Block

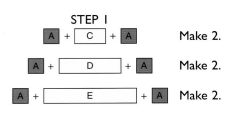

STEP 1

A + C + A   Make 2.

A + D + A   Make 2.

A + E + A   Make 2.

STEP 2

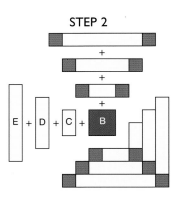

Finished Size	Color	Piece	Cut	Size
8"		A	12	1½" x 1½"
1" unit		B	1	2½" x 2½"
		C	4	1½" x 2½"
		D	4	1½" x 4½"
		E	4	1½" x 6½"
12"		A	12	2" x 2"
1½" unit		B	1	3½" x 3½"
		C	4	2" x 3½"
		D	4	2" x 6½"
		E	4	2" x 9½"

Bear's Paw Block

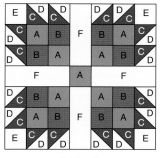

A Block

Finished Size	Color	Piece	Cut	Size
10½"		A	9	2" x 2"
1½" unit		B	8	2" x 2"
		C	8	2⅜" x 2⅜"
		D	8	2⅜" x 2⅜"
		E	4	2" x 2"
		F	4	2" x 5"
14"		A	9	2½" x 2½"
2" unit		B	8	2½" x 2½"
		C	8	2⅞" x 2⅞"
		D	8	2⅞" x 2⅞"
		E	4	2½" x 2½"
		F	4	2½" x 6½"

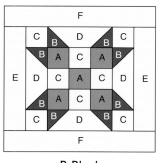

B Block

Finished Size	Color	Piece	Cut	Size
10½"		A	5	2" x 2"
1½" unit		B	8	2" x 2"
		C	8	2" x 2"
		D	4	2" x 5"
		E	2	2" x 8"
		F	2	2" x 11"
14"		A	5	2½" x 2½"
2" unit		B	8	2½" x 2½"
		C	8	2½" x 2½"
		D	4	2½" x 6½"
		E	2	2½" x 10½"
		F	2	2½" x 14½"

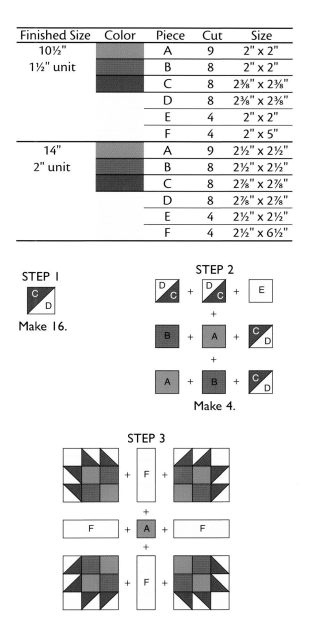

STEP 1
Make 16.

STEP 2
Make 4.

STEP 3

STEP 1
Make 4.

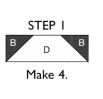

STEP 2
Make 1.

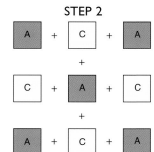

STEP 3

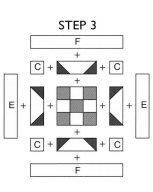

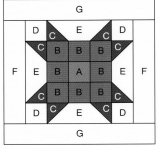

Bear's Paw Block

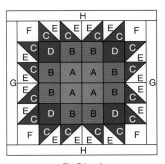

C Block

D Block

Finished Size	Color	Piece	Cut	Size
10½" 1½" unit		A	1	2" x 2"
		B	8	2" x 2"
		C	8	2" x 2"
		D	4	2" x 2"
		E	4	2" x 5"
		F	2	2" x 8"
		G	2	2" x 11"
14" 2" unit		A	1	2½" x 2½"
		B	8	2½" x 2½"
		C	8	2½" x 2½"
		D	4	2½" x 2½"
		E	4	2½" x 6½"
		F	2	2½" x 10½"
		G	2	2½" x 14½"

Finished Size	Color	Piece	Cut	Size
10½" 1½" unit		A	4	2" x 2"
		B	8	2" x 2"
		C	8	2⅜" x 2⅜"
		D	4	2" x 2"
		E	8	2⅜" x 2⅜"
		F	4	2" x 2"
		G	2	1¼" x 9½"
		H	2	1¼" x 11"
14" 2" unit		A	4	2½" x 2½"
		B	8	2½" x 2½"
		C	8	2⅞" x 2⅞"
		D	4	2½" x 2½"
		E	8	2⅞" x 2⅞"
		F	4	2½" x 2½"
		G	2	1½" x 12½"
		H	2	1½" x 14½"

STEP 1

STEP 2

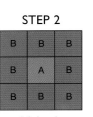

Make 4.

Make 1.

STEP 1

Make 16.

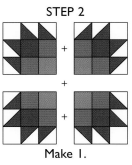

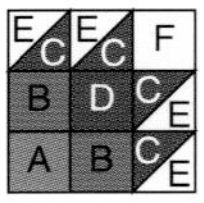

Make 4.

STEP 2

Make 1.

STEP 3

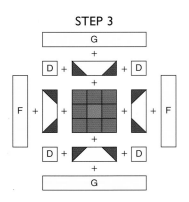

STEP 3

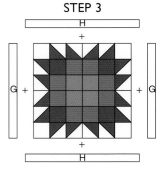

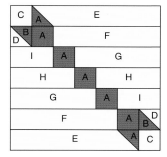

L Block

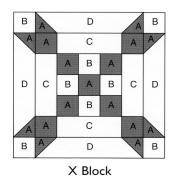

X Block

Finished Size	Color	Piece	Cut	Size
10½"		A	7	2" x 2"
1½" unit		B	1	2⅜" x 2⅜"
		C	2	2" x 2"
		D	1	2⅜" x 2⅜"
		E	2	2" x 9½"
		F	2	2" x 8"
		G	2	2" x 6½"
		H	2	2" x 5"
		I	2	2" x 3½"
14"		A	7	2½" x 2½"
2" unit		B	1	2⅞" x 2⅞"
		C	2	2½" x 2½"
		D	1	2⅞" x 2⅞"
		E	2	2½" x 12½"
		F	2	2½" x 10½"
		G	2	2½" x 8½"
		H	2	2½" x 6½"
		I	2	2½" x 4½"

Finished Size	Color	Piece	Cut	Size
10½"		A	17	2" x 2"
1½" unit		B	8	2" x 2"
		C	4	2" x 5"
		D	4	2" x 8"
14"		A	17	2½" x 2½"
2" unit		B	8	2½" x 2½"
		C	4	2½" x 6½"
		D	4	2½" x 10½"

STEP 1

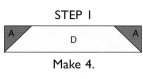

Make 4.

STEP 2

Make 1.

STEP 1

Make 2.

STEP 2

Make 2.

STEP 3

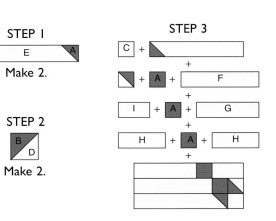

STEP 3

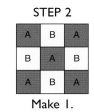

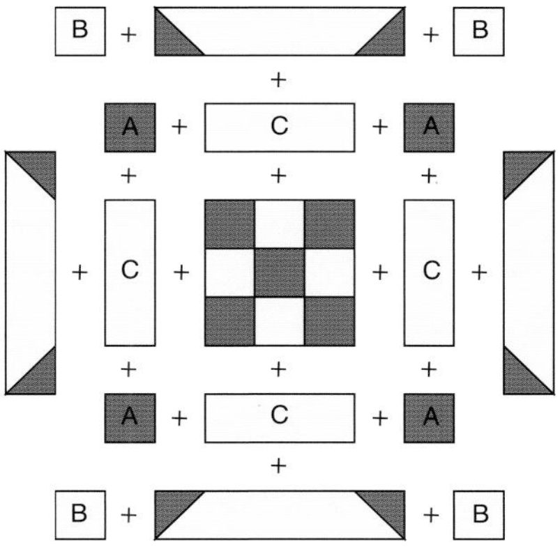

Carpenter's Wheel Block

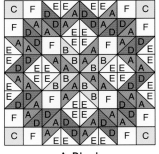

A Block

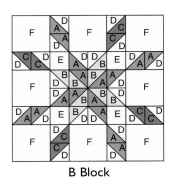

B Block

Finished Size	Color	Piece	Cut	Size
12"		A	16	2⅜" x 2⅜"
1½" unit		B	4	2⅜" x 2⅜"
		C	4	2" x 2"
		D	12	2⅜" x 2⅜"
		E	16	2⅜" x 2⅜"
		F	12	2" x 2"

Finished Size	Color	Piece	Cut	Size
12"		A	8	2⅜" x 2⅜"
1½" unit		B	4	2⅜" x 2⅜"
		C	4	2⅜" x 2⅜"
		D	12	2⅜" x 2⅜"
		E	4	2" x 2"
		F	8	3½" x 3½"

STEP 1

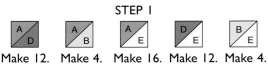

Make 12. Make 4. Make 16. Make 12. Make 4.

STEP 1

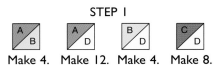

Make 4. Make 12. Make 4. Make 8.

STEP 2

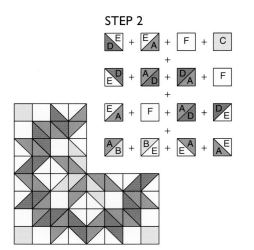

STEP 2

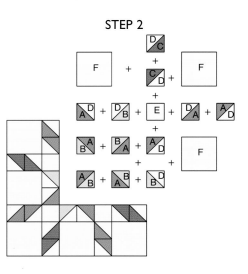

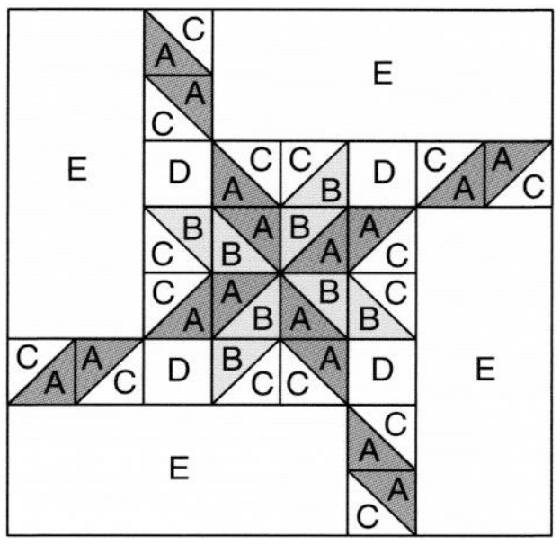

C Block

Finished Size	Color	Piece	Cut	Size
12"	(dark)	A	8	2⅜" x 2⅜"
1½" unit	(light)	B	4	2⅜" x 2⅜"
		C	8	2⅜" x 2⅜"
		D	4	2" x 2"
		E	4	3½" x 8"

STEP 1

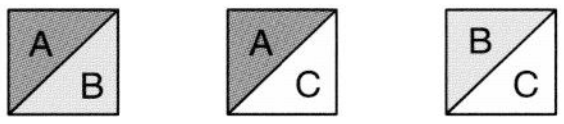

Make 4. Make 12. Make 4.

STEP 2

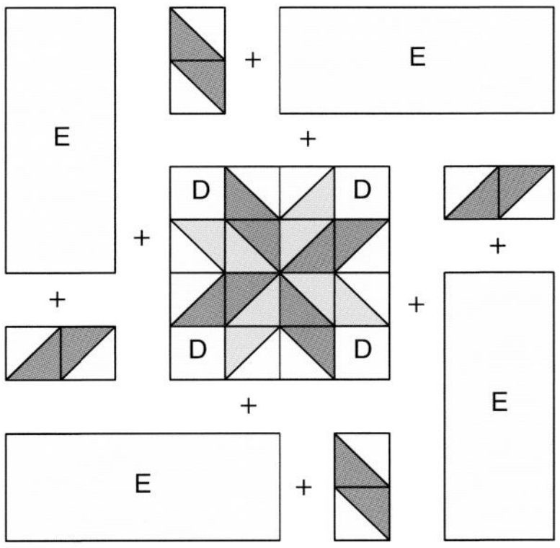

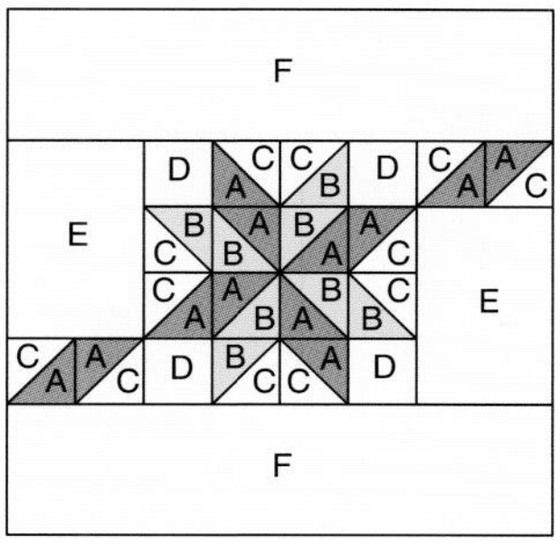

D Block

Finished Size	Color	Piece	Cut	Size
12"	(dark)	A	6	2⅜" x 2⅜"
1½" unit	(light)	B	4	2⅜" x 2⅜"
		C	6	2⅜" x 2⅜"
		D	4	2" x 2"
		E	2	3½" x 5"
		F	2	3½" x 12½"

STEP 1

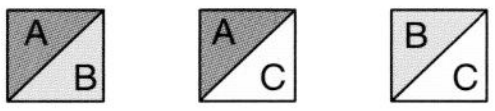

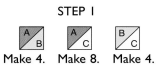

Make 4. Make 8. Make 4.

STEP 2

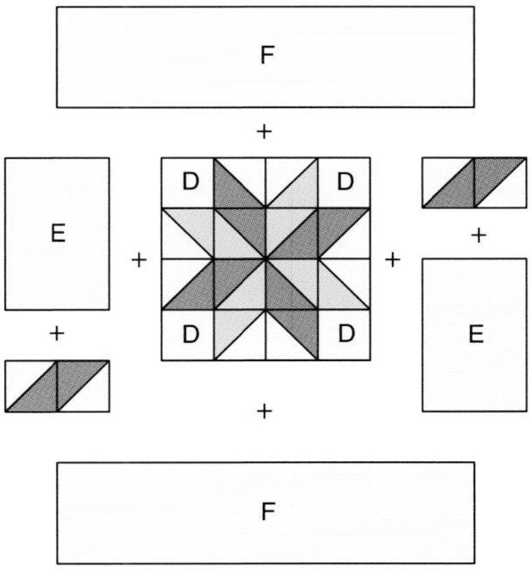

Carpenter's Wheel Block

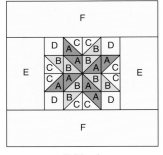

E Block

Finished Size	Color	Piece	Cut	Size
12"		A	4	2⅜" x 2⅜"
1½" unit		B	4	2⅜" x 2⅜"
		C	4	2⅜" x 2⅜"
		D	4	2" x 2"
		E	2	3½" x 6½"
		F	2	3½" x 12½"

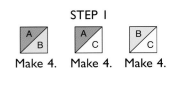

Make 4. Make 4. Make 4.

STEP 2

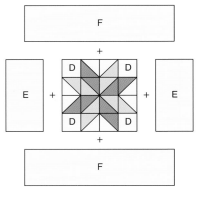

Diamond Star Block

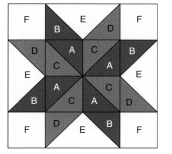

A Block

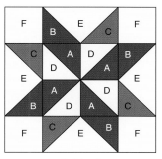

B Block

Finished Size	Color	Piece	Cut	Size
8" 2" unit		A	2	2⅞" x 2⅞"
		B	4	2½" x 2½"
		C	2	2⅞" x 2⅞"
		D	4	2½" x 2½"
		E	4	2½" X 4½"
		F	4	2½" x 2½"
12" 3" unit		A	2	3⅞" x 3⅞"
		B	4	3½" x 3½"
		C	2	3⅞" x 3⅞"
		D	4	3½" x 3½"
		E	4	3½" x 6½"
		F	4	3½" x 3½"

Finished Size	Color	Piece	Cut	Size
8" 2" unit		A	2	2⅞" x 2⅞"
		B	4	2½" x 2½"
		C	4	2½" x 2½"
		D	2	2⅞" x 2⅞"
		E	4	2½" x 4½"
		F	4	2½" x 2½"
12" 3" unit		A	2	3⅞" x 3⅞"
		B	4	3½" x 3½"
		C	4	3½" x 3½"
		D	2	3⅞" x 3⅞"
		E	4	3½" x 6½"
		F	4	3½" x 3½"

STEP 1

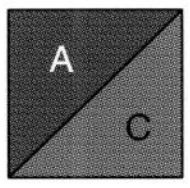

Make 4.

STEP 2

Make 1.

STEP 3

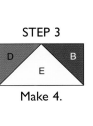

Make 4.

STEP 4

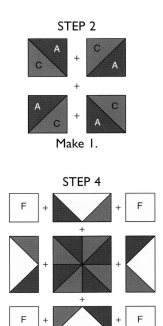

STEP 1

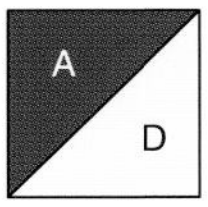

Make 4.

STEP 2

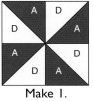

Make 1.

STEP 3

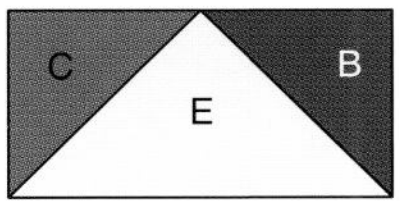

Make 4.

STEP 4

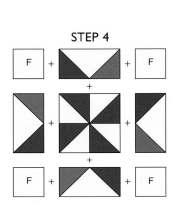

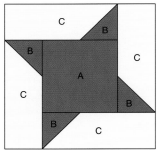

Diamond Star Block

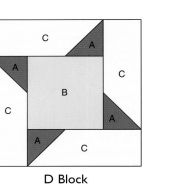

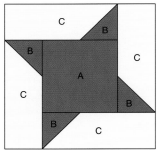

C Block

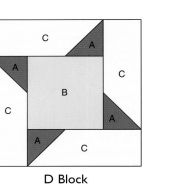

D Block

Finished Size	Color	Piece	Cut	Size
8"		A	1	4½" x 4½"
2" unit		B	4	2½" x 2½"
		C	4	2½" x 6½"
12"		A	1	6½" x 6½"
3" unit		B	4	3½" x 3½"
		C	4	3½" x 9½"

Finished Size	Color	Piece	Cut	Size
8"		A	4	2½" x 2½"
2" unit		B	1	4½" x 4½"
		C	4	2½" x 6½"
12"		A	4	3½" x 3½"
3" unit		B	1	6½" x 6½"
		C	4	3½" x 9½"

STEP 1

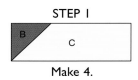

Make 4.

STEP 1

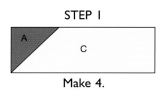

Make 4.

STEP 2

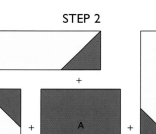

STEP 2

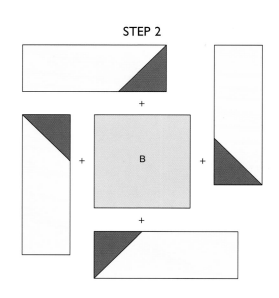

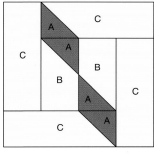

E Block

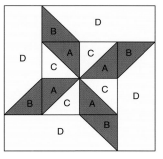

F Block

Finished Size	Color	Piece	Cut	Size
8"		A	4	2½" x 2½"
2" unit		B	2	2½" x 4½"
		C	4	2½" x 6½"
12"		A	4	3½" x 3½"
3" unit		B	2	3½" x 6½"
		C	4	3½" x 9½"

Finished Size	Color	Piece	Cut	Size
8"		A	2	2⅞" x 2⅞"
2" unit		B	4	2½" x 2½"
		C	2	2⅞" x 2⅞"
		D	4	2½" x 6½"
12"		A	2	3⅞" x 3⅞"
3" unit		B	4	3½" x 3½"
		C	2	3⅞" x 3⅞"
		D	4	3½" x 9½"

STEP 1

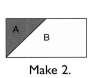

Make 2. 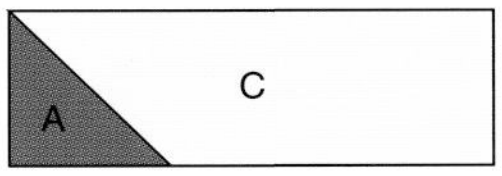   Make 2.

STEP 1

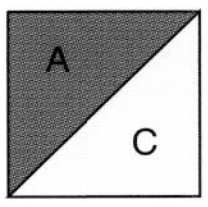

Make 4.

STEP 2

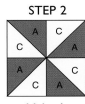

Make 1.

STEP 3

Make 4.

STEP 2

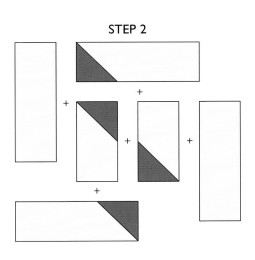

STEP 4

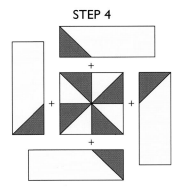

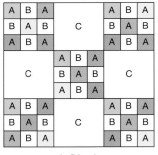

Double Nine-Patch Block

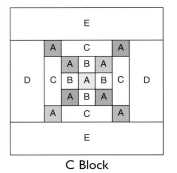

A Block

Finished Size	Color	Piece	Cut	Size
9"		A	25	1½" x 1½"
1" unit		B	20	1½" x 1½"
		C	4	3½" x 3½"

STEP 1

Make 5 Nine-Patches.

A + B + A
+
B + A + B
+
A + B + A

STEP 2

+ C +

+

B Block

Finished Size	Color	Piece	Cut	Size
9"		A	20	1½" x 1½"
1" unit		B	25	1½" x 1½"
		C	4	3½" x 3½"

STEP 1

Make 5.

B + A + B
+
A + B + A
+
B + A + B

STEP 2

+ C +

+

C Block

Finished Size	Color	Piece	Cut	Size
9"		A	9	1½" x 1½"
1" unit		B	4	1½" x 1½"
		C	4	1½" x 3½"
		D	2	2½" x 5½"
		E	2	2½" x 9½"

STEP 1

A + C + A

Make 2.

STEP 2

A	B	A
B	A	B
A	B	A

Make 1.

STEP 3

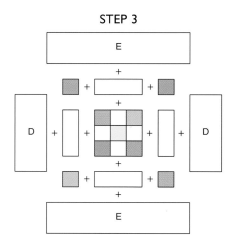

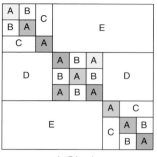

L Block

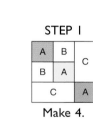

X Block

Finished Size	Color	Piece	Cut	Size
9"		A	11	1½" x 1½"
1" unit		B	8	1½" x 1½"
		C	4	1½" x 2½"
		D	2	3½" x 3½"
		E	2	3½" x 6½"

Finished Size	Color	Piece	Cut	Size
9"		A	17	1½" x 1½"
1" unit		B	12	1½" x 1½"
		C	8	1½" x 2½"
		D	4	3½" x 3½"

STEP 1   STEP 2

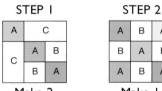

Make 2.   Make 1.

STEP 1   STEP 2

Make 4.   Make 1.

STEP 3

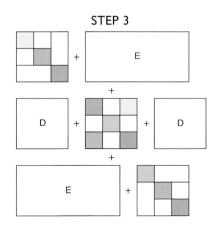

STEP 3

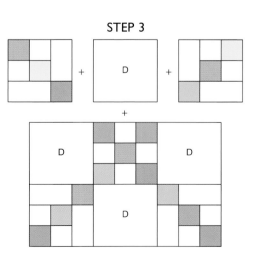

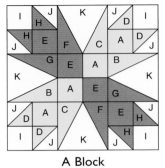

A Block

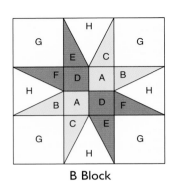

B Block

Finished Size	Color	Piece	Cut	Size
9"		A	4	2" x 2"
1½" unit		B	2	Template 1
		C	2	Template 1R
		D	2	2⅜" x 2⅜"
		E	4	2" x 2"
		F	2	Template 1
		G	2	Template 1R
		H	2	2⅜" x 2⅜"
		I	4	2" x 2"
		J	4	2⅜" x 2⅜"
		K	4	Template 2

Finished Size	Color	Piece	Cut	Size
9"		A	2	2" x 2"
1½" unit		B	2	Template 1
		C	2	Template 1R
		D	2	2" x 2"
		E	2	Template 1
		F	2	Template 1R
		G	4	3½" x 3½"
		H	4	Template 2

STEP 1

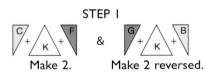

C + K + F & G + K + B

Make 2. Make 2 reversed.

STEP 2

Make 1.

STEP 1

Make 2. Make 2.

STEP 2

Make 1.

STEP 3

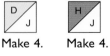

Make 4. Make 4.

STEP 4

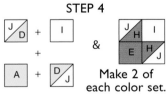

&

Make 2 of each color set.

STEP 3

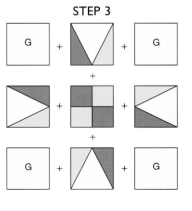

STEP 5

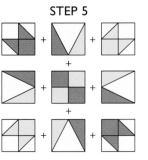

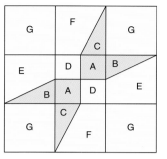

C Block

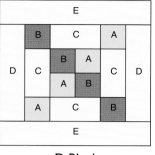

D Block

Finished Size	Color	Piece	Cut	Size
9"		A	2	2" x 2"
1½" unit		B	2	Template 1
		C	2	Template 1R
		D	2	2" x 2"
		E	2	Template 3
		F	2	Template 3R
		G	4	3½" x 3½"

Finished Size	Color	Piece	Cut	Size
9"		A	4	2" x 2"
1½" unit		B	4	2" x 2"
		C	4	2" x 3½"
		D	2	2" x 6½"
		E	2	2" x 9½"

STEP 1

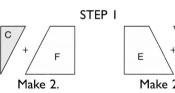

Make 2.　Make 2.

STEP 2

Make 1.

STEP 3

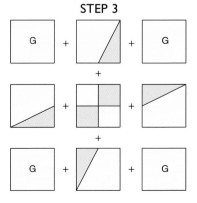

STEP 1

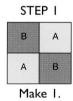

Make 1.

STEP 2

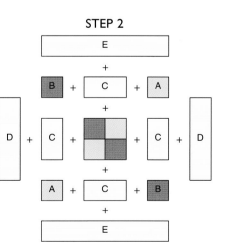

Fifty-four Forty or Fight Block

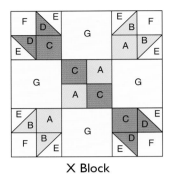

X Block

Finished Size	Color	Piece	Cut	Size
9"		A	4	2" x 2"
1½" unit		B	2	2⅜" x 2⅜"
		C	4	2" x 2"
		D	2	2⅜"x 2⅜"
		E	4	2⅜" x 2⅜"
		F	4	2" x 2"
		G	4	3½" x 3½"

STEP 1

Make 1.

STEP 2

Make 4.   Make 4.

STEP 3

Make 2 of each color.

STEP 4

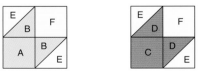

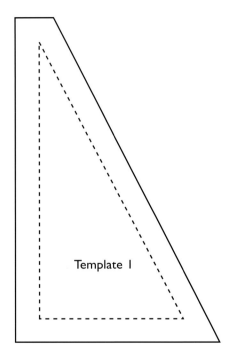

Template 1

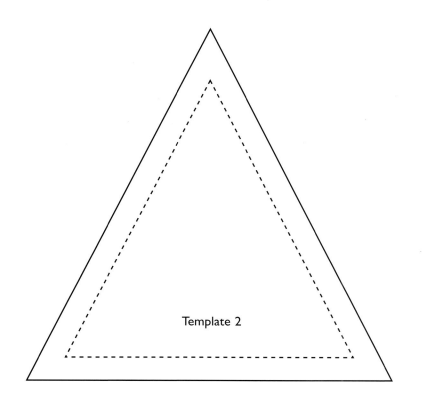

Template 2

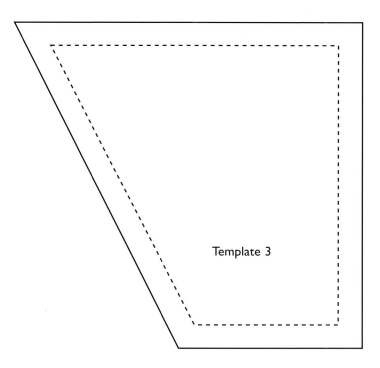

Template 3

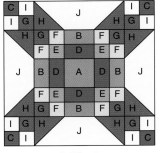

Game Cocks Block

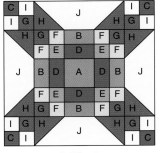

A Block

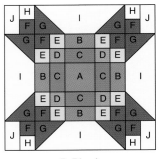

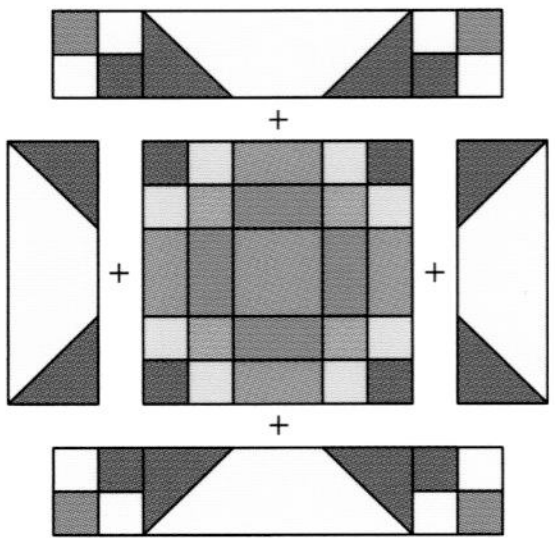

B Block

Finished Size	Color	Piece	Cut	Size
10"		A	1	2½" x 2½"
1" unit		B	4	1½" x 2½"
		C	4	1½" x 1½"
		D	4	1½" x 2½"
		E	4	1½" x 1½"
		F	8	1½" x 1½"
		G	8	1½" x 1½"
		H	8	2½" x 2½"
		I	8	1½" x 1½"
		J	4	2½" x 6½"

Finished Size	Color	Piece	Cut	Size
10"		A	1	2½" x 2½"
1" unit		B	4	1½" x 2½"
		C	4	1½" x 2½"
		D	4	1½" x 1½"
		E	8	1½" x 1½"
		F	8	1½" x 1½"
		G	8	2½" x 2½"
		H	4	1½" x 1½"
		I	4	2½" x 6½"
		J	4	1½" x 2½"

STEP 1

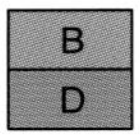

B
D

Make 4.

STEP 2

C I
I G

Make 4.

STEP 3

G F
F E

Make 4.

STEP 4

H   J   H

Make 4.

STEP 5

C I   I C
I G H J H G I

Make 2.

STEP 6

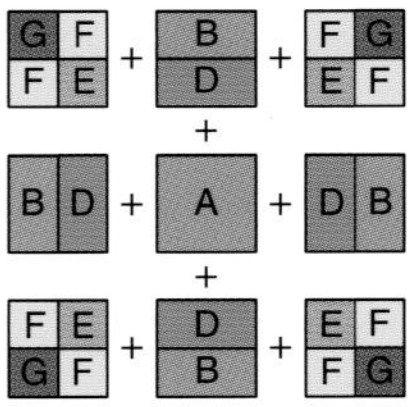

G F + B + F G
F E   D   E F
  +
B D + A + D B
  +
F E + D + E F
G F   B   F G

Make 1.

Make same as A Block, but in
Step 2 substitute background
J rectangles for C/I units in
four outside corners.

STEP 7

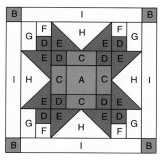

C Block

Finished Size	Color	Piece	Cut	Size
10"		A	1	2½" x 2½"
1" unit		B	4	1½" x 1½"
		C	4	1½" x 2½"
		D	8	1½" x 1½"
		E	8	2½" x 2½"
		F	4	1½" x 1½"
		G	4	1½" x 2½"
		H	4	2½" x 4½"
		I	4	1½" x 8½"

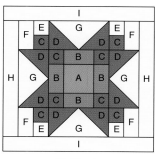

D Block

Finished Size	Color	Piece	Cut	Size
10"		A	1	2½" x 2½"
1" unit		B	4	1½" x 2½"
		C	8	1½" x 1½"
		D	8	2½" x 2½"
		E	4	1½" x 1½"
		F	4	1½" x 2½"
		G	4	2½" x 4½"
		H	2	1½" x 8½"
		I	2	1½" x 10½"

Make same as C Block except in outer row. Replace 4 green 1½" x 1½" squares and 2 background 1½" x 8½" rectangles with 2 background 1½" x 10½" rectangles.

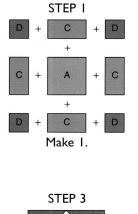

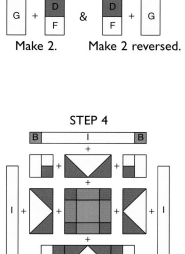

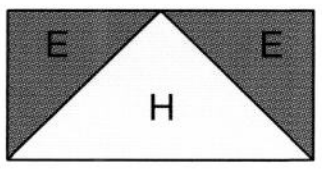

Game Cocks Block

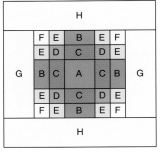

E Block

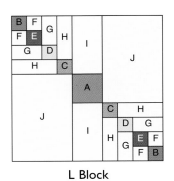

L Block

Finished Size	Color	Piece	Cut	Size
10"		A	1	2½" x 2½"
1" unit		B	4	1½" x 2½"
		C	4	1½" x 2½"
		D	4	1½" x 1½"
		E	8	1½" x 1½"
		F	4	1½" x 1½"
		G	2	2½" x 6½"
		H	2	2½" x 10½"

Finished Size	Color	Piece	Cut	Size
10"		A	1	2½" x 2½"
1" unit		B	2	1½" x 1½"
		C	2	1½" x 1½"
		D	2	1½" x 1½"
		E	2	1½" x 1½"
		F	4	1½" x 1½"
		G	4	1½" x 2½"
		H	4	1½" x 3½"
		I	2	2½" x 4½"
		J	2	4½" x 6½"

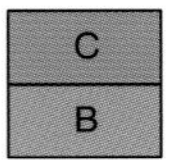

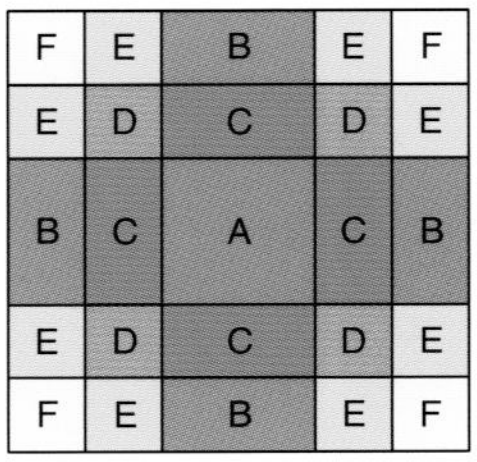

STEP 1   **STEP 2**   **STEP 3**

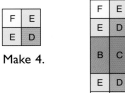

Make 4.   Make 4.   Make 1.

STEP 4

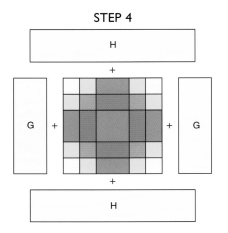

STEP 1

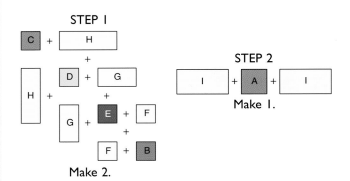

Make 2.

STEP 2

I + A + I

Make 1.

STEP 3

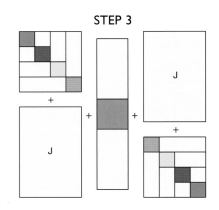

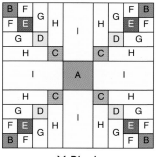

X Block

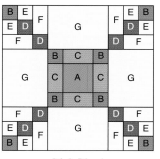

X-1 Block

Finished Size	Color	Piece	Cut	Size
10"		A	1	2½" x 2½"
1" unit		B	4	1½" x 1½"
		C	4	1½" x 1½"
		D	4	1½" x 1½"
		E	4	1½" x 1½"
		F	8	1½" x 1½"
		G	8	1½" x 2½"
		H	8	1½" x 3½"
		I	4	2½" x 4½"

Finished Size	Color	Piece	Cut	Size
10"		A	1	2½" x 2½"
1" unit		B	8	1½" x 1½"
		C	4	1½" x 2½"
		D	8	1½" x 1½"
		E	8	1½" x 1½"
		F	8	1½" x 2½"
		G	4	3½" x 4½"

STEP 1

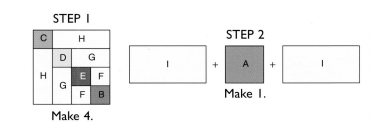

Make 4.

Make 1.

STEP 3

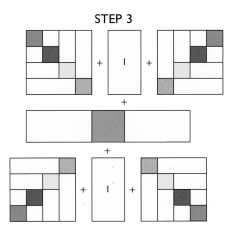

STEP 1

STEP 2

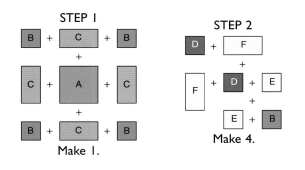

Make 1.

Make 4.

STEP 3

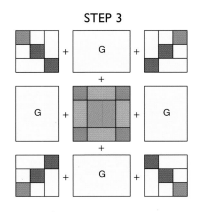

Hovering Hawks Block

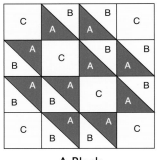

A Block

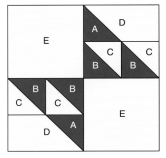

B Block

Finished Size	Color	Piece	Cut	Size
8"		A	5	2⅞" x 2⅞"
2" unit		B	5	2⅞" x 2⅞"
		C	6	2½" x 2½"
12"		A	5	3⅞" x 3⅞"
3" unit		B	5	3⅞" x 3⅞"
		C	6	3½" x 3½"

Finished Size	Color	Piece	Cut	Size
8"		A	2	2½" x 2½"
2" unit		B	2	2⅞" x 2⅞"
		C	2	2⅞" x 2⅞"
		D	2	2½" x 4½"
		E	2	4½" x 4½"
12"		A	2	3½" x 3½"
3" unit		B	2	3⅞" x 3⅞"
		C	2	3⅞" x 3⅞"
		D	2	3½" x 6½"
		E	2	6½" x 6½"

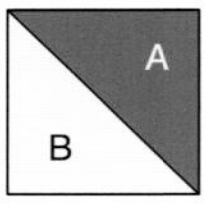

STEP 1

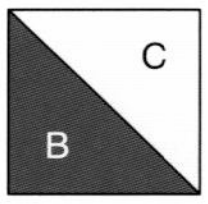

Make 10.

STEP 2

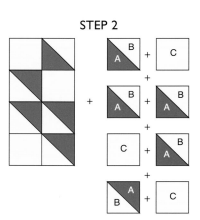

STEP 1

Make 4.

STEP 2

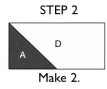

Make 2.

STEP 3

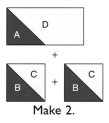

Make 2.

STEP 4

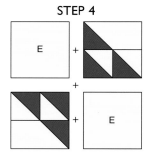

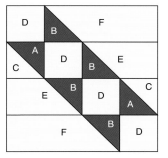

L Block

Finished Size	Color	Piece	Cut	Size
8"		A	1	2⅞" x 2⅞"
2" unit		B	4	2½" x 2½"
		C	1	2⅞" x 2⅞"
		D	4	2½" x 2½"
		E	2	2½" x 4½"
		F	2	2½" x 6½"
12"		A	1	3⅞" x 3⅞"
3" unit		B	4	3½" x 3½"
		C	1	3⅞" x 3⅞"
		D	4	3½" x 3½"
		E	2	3½" x 6½"
		F	2	3½" x 9½"

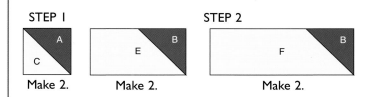

STEP 1

Make 2.

STEP 2

Make 2.

Make 2.

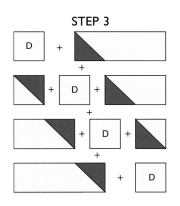

STEP 3

Priscilla's Dream Block

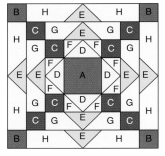

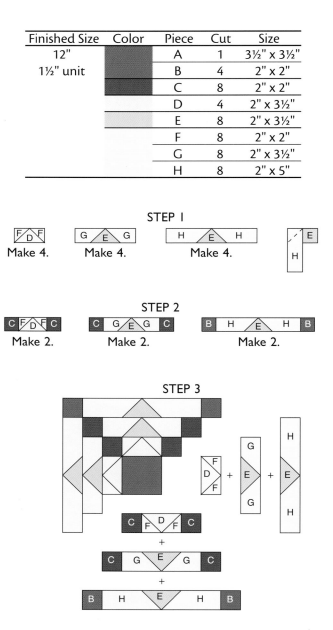

A Block

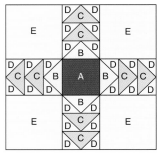

B Block

Finished Size	Color	Piece	Cut	Size
12"		A	1	3½" x 3½"
1½" unit		B	4	2" x 2"
		C	8	2" x 2"
		D	4	2" x 3½"
		E	8	2" x 3½"
		F	8	2" x 2"
		G	8	2" x 3½"
		H	8	2" x 5"

Finished Size	Color	Piece	Cut	Size
12"		A	1	3½" x 3½"
1½" unit		B	4	2" x 3½"
		C	8	2" x 3½"
		D	24	2" x 2"
		E	4	5" x 5"

STEP 1

F D F
Make 4.

G E G
Make 4.

H E H
Make 4.

E
H
(Make 4.)

STEP 1

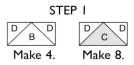

D B D
Make 4.

D C D
Make 8.

STEP 2

C F D F C
Make 2.

C G E G C
Make 2.

B H E H B
Make 2.

STEP 3

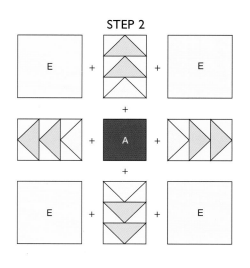

STEP 2

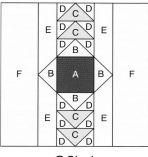

C Block

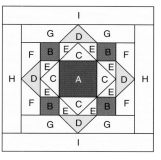

D Block

Finished Size	Color	Piece	Cut	Size
12"		A	1	3½" x 3½"
1½" unit		B	4	2" x 3½"
		C	4	2" x 3½"
		D	12	2" x 2"
		E	4	2" x 6½"
		F	2	3½" x 12½"

Finished Size	Color	Piece	Cut	Size
12"		A	1	3½" x 3½"
1½" unit		B	4	2" x 2"
		C	4	2" x 3½"
		D	4	2" x 3½"
		E	8	2" x 2"
		F	4	2" x 3½"
		G	4	2" x 5"
		H	2	2" x 9½"
		I	2	2" x 12½"

STEP 1

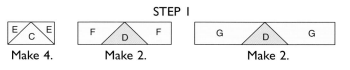

Make 4.　　Make 2.　　Make 2.

STEP 1

Make 2.　Make 4.　Make 2.

STEP 2

Make 2.

STEP 2

Make 2.

STEP 3

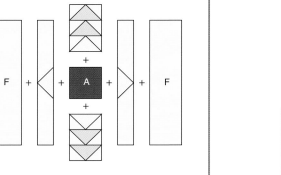

STEP 3

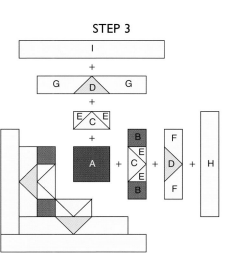

Priscilla's Dream Block

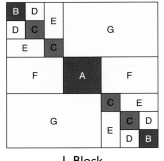

L Block

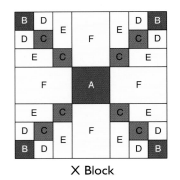

X Block

Finished Size	Color	Piece	Cut	Size
12"		A	1	3½" x 3½"
1½" unit		B	2	2" x 2"
		C	4	2" x 2"
		D	4	2" x 2"
		E	4	2" x 3½"
		F	2	3½" x 5"
		G	2	5" x 8"

Finished Size	Color	Piece	Cut	Size
12"		A	1	3½" x 3½"
1½" unit		B	4	2" x 2"
		C	8	2" x 2"
		D	8	2" x 2"
		E	8	2" x 3½"
		F	4	3½" x 5"

STEP 1

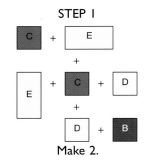

Make 2.

STEP 1

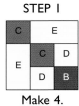

Make 4.

STEP 2

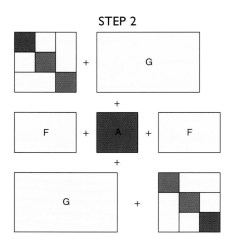

STEP 2

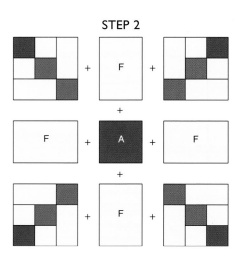

Weathervane Block

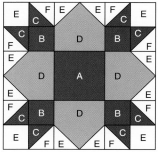

A Block

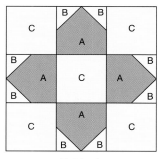

B Block

Finished Size	Color	Piece	Cut	Size
9"		A	1	3½" x 3½"
1½" unit		B	4	2" x 2"
		C	4	2⅜" x 2⅜"
		D	4	3½" x 3½"
		E	12	2" x 2"
		F	4	2⅜" x 2⅜"
12"		A	1	4½" x 4½"
2" unit		B	4	2½" x 2½"
		C	4	2⅞" x 2⅞"
		D	4	4½" x 4½"
		E	12	2½" x 2½"
		F	4	2⅞" x 2⅞"

Finished Size	Color	Piece	Cut	Size
9"		A	4	3½" x 3½"
1½" unit		B	8	2" x 2"
		C	5	3½" x 3½"
12"		A	4	4½" x 4½"
2" unit		B	8	2½" x 2½"
		C	5	4½" x 4½"

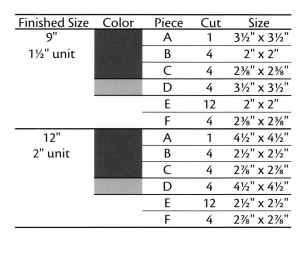

STEP 1

Make 8.

STEP 2

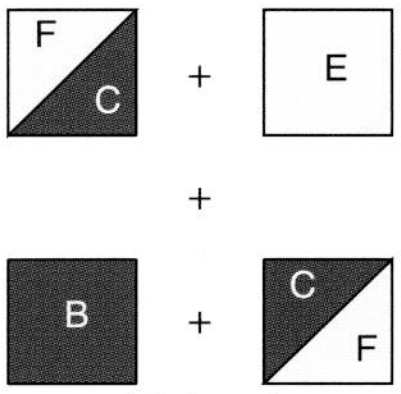

Make 4.

STEP 3

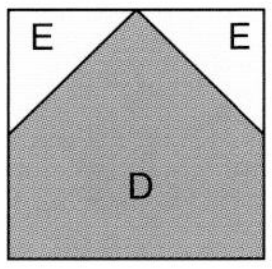

Make 4.

STEP 4

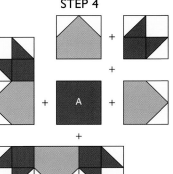

STEP 1

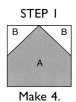

Make 4.

STEP 2

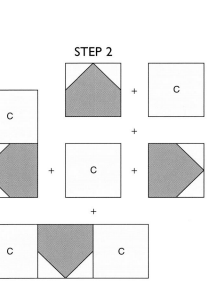

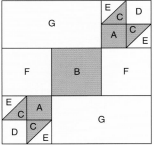

L Block

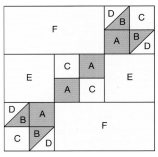

L-1 Block

Finished Size	Color	Piece	Cut	Size
9"		A	2	2" x 2"
1½" unit		B	1	3½" x 3½"
		C	2	2⅜" x 2⅜"
		D	2	2" x 2"
		E	2	2⅜" x 2⅜"
		F	2	3½" x 3½"
		G	2	3½" x 6½"
12"		A	2	2½" x 2½"
2" unit		B	1	4½" x 4½"
		C	2	2⅞" x 2⅞"
		D	2	2½" x 2½"
		E	2	2⅞" x 2⅞"
		F	2	4½" x 4½"
		G	2	4½" x 8½"

Finished Size	Color	Piece	Cut	Size
9"		A	4	2" x 2"
1½" unit		B	2	2⅜" x 2⅜"
		C	4	2" x 2"
		D	2	2⅜" x 2⅜"
		E	2	3½" x 3½"
		F	2	3½" x 6½"
12"		A	4	2½" x 2½"
2" unit		B	2	2⅞" x 2⅞"
		C	4	2½" x 2½"
		D	2	2⅞" x 2⅞"
		E	2	4½" x 4½"
		F	2	4½" x 8½"

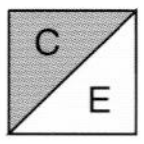

STEP 1

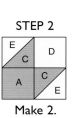

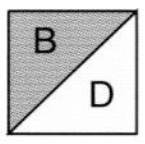

Make 4.

STEP 2

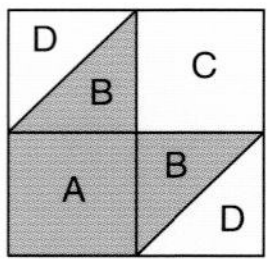

Make 2.

STEP 3

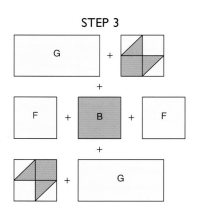

STEP 1

Make 4.

STEP 2

Make 2.

STEP 3

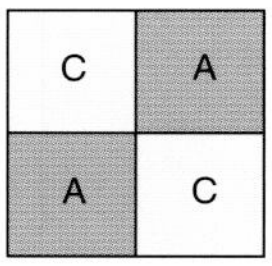

Make 1.

STEP 4

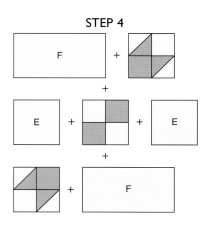

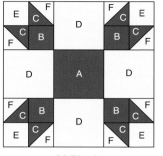

X Block

Finished Size	Color	Piece	Cut	Size
9"		A	1	3½" x 3½"
1½" unit		B	4	2" x 2"
		C	4	2⅜" x 2⅜"
		D	4	3½" x 3½"
		E	4	2" x 2"
		F	4	2⅜" x 2⅜"
12"		A	1	4½" x 4½"
2" unit		B	4	2½" x 2½"
		C	4	2⅞" x 2⅞"
		D	4	4½" x 4½"
		E	4	2½" x 2½"
		F	4	2⅞" x 2⅞"

STEP 1

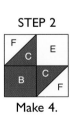

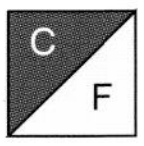

Make 8.

STEP 2

F C E
B C F

Make 4.

STEP 3

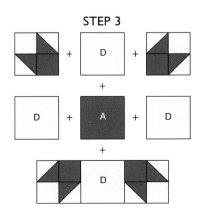

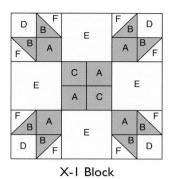

X-1 Block

Finished Size	Color	Piece	Cut	Size
9"		A	6	2" x 2"
1½" unit		B	4	2⅜" x 2⅜"
		C	2	2" x 2"
		D	4	2" x 2"
		E	4	3½" x 3½"
		F	4	2⅜" x 2⅜"
12"		A	6	2½" x 2½"
2" unit		B	4	2⅞" x 2⅞"
		C	2	2½" x 2½"
		D	4	2½" x 2½"
		E	4	4½" x 4½"
		F	4	2⅞" x 2⅞"

STEP 1

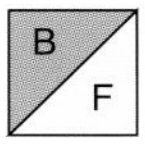

B F

Make 8.

STEP 2

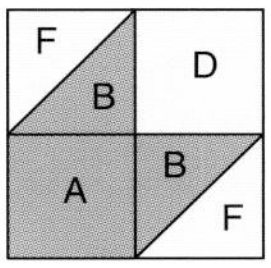

F B D
A B F

Make 4.

STEP 3

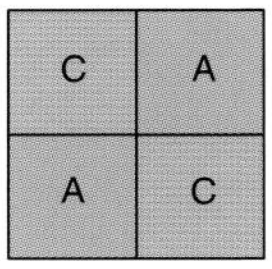

C A
A C

Make 1.

STEP 4

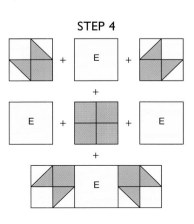

1 x 3 Horizontal Setting

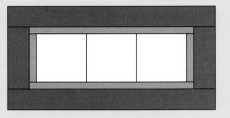

Finished Block	Inner Border	Outer Border	Finished Size of Quilt
8"	1"	2"	14" x 30"
9"	1"	3"	17" x 35"
10"	2"	4"	22" x 42"
10½"	1½"	3"	19½" x 40½"
12"	2"	4"	24" x 48"
14"	2"	6"	30" x 58"

FABRIC REQUIREMENTS (in yards)

Block	Inner Border	Outer Border	Binding	Backing
8"	¼	¼	⅜	½
9"	¼	⅜	⅜	⅝
10"	⅜	⅝	⅜	1⅜
10½"	¼	⅜	⅜	1¼
12"	⅜	¾	⅜	1⅝
14"	⅜	1¼	½	1⅞

CUTTING INSTRUCTIONS

Block	Inner Border	Outer Border	Binding
8"	1½" x 8½"	2½" x 10½"	3
	1½" x 26½"	2½" x 30½"	
9"	1½" x 9½"	3½" x 11½"	3
	1½" x 29½"	3½" x 35½"	
10"	2½" x 10½"	4½" x 14½"	4
	2½" x 34½"	4½" x 42½"**	
10½"	2" x 11"	3½" x 14"	4
	2" x 35"	3½" x 41"**	
12"	2½" x 12½"	4½" x 16½"	4
	2½" x 40½"	4½" x 48½"**	
14"	2½" x 14½"	6½" x 18½"	5
	2½" x 46½"**	6½" x 58½"**	

** *Piece fabric strips to get needed length.*
For binding, cut the number of 2½" x width of fabric strips listed under binding.

Cut 2 strips each length for inner and outer borders.

3 x 3 Horizontal Setting

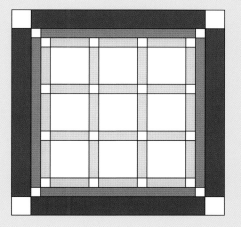

Finished Block	Sash.	Sash. Block	Inner Border	Corner Block	Outer Border	Corner Block	Size of Quilt
8"	2"	2"	2"	2"	4"	4"	44" x 44"
9"	2"	2"	2"	2"	4"	4"	47" x 47"
10"	2"	2"	2"	2"	4"	4"	50" x 50"
10½"	1½"	1½"	2"	2"	4"	4"	49½" x 49½"
12"	2"	2"	2"	2"	4"	4"	56" x 56"
14"	2"	2"	2"	2"	6"	6"	66" x 66"

FABRIC REQUIREMENTS (in yards)

Block	Sash.	Sash. Block	Inner Border	Corner Block	Outer Border	Corner Block	Binding	Backing
8"	⅝	¼	⅜	⅛	⅔	¼	½	3
9"	⅝	¼	⅜	⅛	⅔	¼	⅝	3
10"	⅔	¼	⅜	⅛	¾	¼	⅝	3¼
10½"	½	⅛	⅜	⅛	¾	¼	⅝	3¼
12"	¾	¼	½	⅛	¾	¼	⅝	3½
14"	1	¼	½	⅛	1¼	¼	⅔	4

CUTTING INSTRUCTIONS

Block	Sashing	Sashing Squares	Inner Border	Squares	Outer Border	Squares	Binding
8"	2½" x 8½"	2½"	2½" x 32½"	2½"	4½" x 36½"	4½"	5
9"	2½" x 9½"	2½"	2½" x 35½"	2½"	4½" x 39½"	4½"	6
10"	2½" x 10½"	2½"	2½" x 38½"	2½"	4½" x 42½"**	4½"	6
10½"	2" x 11"	2"	2½" x 40"	2½"	4½" x 44"**	4½"	6
12"	2½" x 12½"	2½"	2½" x 44½"**	2½"	4½" X 48½"**	4½"	7
14"	2½" x 14½"	2½"	2½" x 50½"**	2½"	6½" x 54½"**	6½"	8

** Piece fabric strips to get needed length.
For binding cut the number of 2½" x width of fabric strips listed under binding.

Cut 24 strips the length for sashing, and 16 squares for sashing blocks.

Cut 4 strips each length for inner and outer borders and 4 squares for corners.

3 x 5 Horizontal Setting

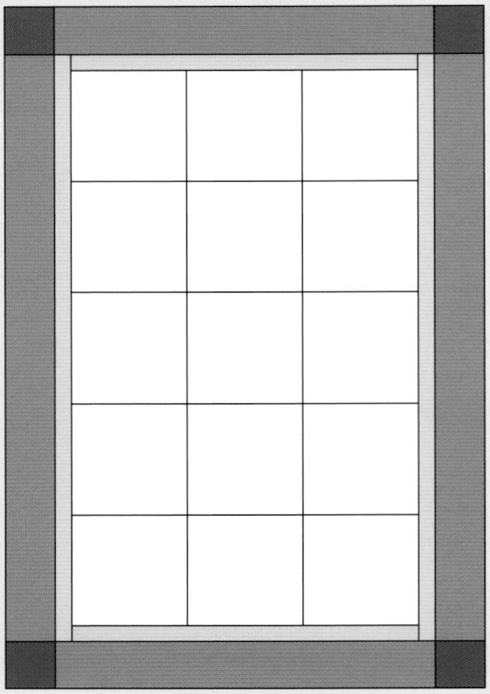

Finished Block	Inner Border	Outer Border	Corner Squares	Finished Size of Quilt
8"	2"	4"	4"	36" x 52"
9"	1½"	3"	3"	36" x 54"
10"	2"	3½"	3½"	41" x 61"
10½"	3½"	5"	5"	48½" x 69½"
12"	2"	4"	4"	48" x 72"
14"	2"	4"	4"	54" x 82"

FABRIC REQUIREMENTS (in yards)

Block	Inner Border	Outer Border	Corner Squares	Binding	Backing
8"	⅜	⅔	¼	½	1⅔
9"	⅜	⅝	¼	½	1⅔
10"	½	¾	¼	⅝	3⅝
10½"	⅞	1¼	¼	⅝	4⅛
12"	½	1	¼	⅝	4⅓
14"	⅝	1¼	¼	⅔	5

CUTTING INSTRUCTIONS

Block	Inner Border	Outer Border	Corner Squares	Binding
8"	2½" x 24½"	4½" x 28½"	4½"	5
	2½" x 44½"**	4½" x 44½"**		
9"	2" x 27½"	3½" x 30½"	3½"	5
	2" x 48½"**	3½" x 48½"**		
10"	2½" x 30½"	4" x 34½"	4"	6
	2½" x 54½"**	4" x 54½"**		
10½"	4" x 32"	5½" x 39"	5½"	7
	4" x 60"**	5½" x 60"**		
12"	2½" x 36½"	4½" x 40½"**	4½"	7
	2½" x 64½"**	4½" x 64½"**		
14"	2½" x 42½"**	4½" x 46½"**	4½"	8
	2½" x 74½"**	4½" x 74½"**		

**Piece fabric strips to get needed length.
For binding cut the number of 2½" x width of fabric strips listed under binding.

Cut 2 strips each length for inner and outer borders, and 4 squares for corners.

4 x 4 Horizontal Setting

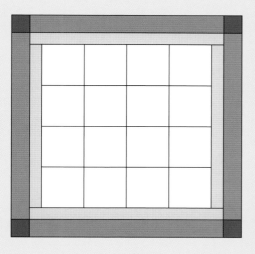

Finished Block	Inner Border	Outer Border	Corner Squares	Finished Size of Quilt
8"	2"	4"	4"	44" x 44"
9"	3"	4½"	4½"	51" x 51"
10"	2"	4"	4"	52" x 52"
10½"	2"	4"	4"	54" x 54"
12"	2"	4"	4"	60" x 60"
14"	2"	6"	6"	72" x 72"

FABRIC REQUIREMENTS (in yards)

Block	Inner Border	Outer Border	Corner Squares	Binding	Backing
8"	⅜	⅝	¼	½	3
9"	⅝	⅞	¼	⅝	3¼
10"	½	¾	¼	⅝	3¼
10½"	½	¾	¼	⅝	3½
12"	½	1	¼	⅔	3¾
14"	⅝	1½	¼	⅔	4½

CUTTING INSTRUCTIONS

Block	Inner Border	Outer Border	Corner Squares	Binding
8"	2½" x 32½"	4½" x 36½"	4½"	5
	2½" x 36½"			
9"	3½" x 36½"	5" x 42½"**	5"	6
	3½" x 42½"**			
10"	2½" x 40½"	4½" x 44½"**	4½"	6
	2½" x 44½"**			
10½"	2½" x 42½"**	4½" x 46½"**	4½"	7
	2½" x 46½"**			
12"	2½" x 48½"**	4½" x 52½"**	4½"	7
	2½" x 52½"			
14"	2½" x 56½"**	6½" x 60½"**	6½"	8
	2½" x 60½"**			

*Piece fabric strips to get needed length.
For binding cut the number of 2½" x width of fabric strips listed under binding.

Cut 2 strips each length for inner border and 4 strips the length for outer border, and 4 squares for corners.

5x5 Horizontal Setting

Finished Block	Sash.	Sash. Block	Inner Border	Corner Block	Outer Border	Corner Block	Size of Quilt
8"	2"	2"	2"	2"	4"	4"	64" x 64"
9"	1½	1½	3"	3"	6"	6"	72" x 72"
10"	2"	2"	3"	3"	4"	4"	76" x 76"
10½"	2"	2"	3"	3"	4"	4"	78½" x 78½"
12"	2"	2"	2"	2"	6"	6"	88" x 88"
14"	2"	2"	3"	3"	6"	6"	100" x 100"

FABRIC REQUIREMENTS (in yards)

Block	Sash.	Sash. Block	Inner Border	Corner Block	Outer Border	Corner Block	Binding	Backing
8"	1⅛	¼	⅝	¼	1	¼	⅝	4
9"	1¼	¼	¾	¼	1½	¼	⅔	4½
10"	1½	¼	⅞	¼	1¼	¼	⅔	4¾
10½"	1½	¼	⅞	¼	1¼	¼	¾	7¼
12"	1½	¼	⅔	¼	1⅝	¼	⅞	7¾
14"	2¼	¼	1	¼	2	¼	⅞	9

CUTTING INSTRUCTIONS

Block	Sashing	Sashing Squares	Inner Border	Squares	Outer Border**	Squares	Binding
8"	2½" x 8½"	2½"	2½" x 52½"**	2½"	4½" x 56½"**	4½"	7
9"	2" x 9½"	2"	3½" x 54½"**	3½"	6½" x 60½"**	6½"	8
10"	2½" x 10½"	2½"	3½" x 62½"**	3½"	4½" x 68½"**	4½"	8
10½"	2½" x 11"	2½"	3½" x 65"**	3½"	4½" x 71"**	4½"	9
12"	2½" x 12½"	2½"	2½" x 72½"**	2½"	6½" x 76½"**	6½"	10
14"	2½" x 14½"	2½"	3½" x 82½"**	3½"	6½" x 88½"**	6½"	11

* Piece fabric strips to get needed length.
For binding cut the number of 2½" x width of fabric strips listed under binding.

Cut 60 strips the length for sashing, and 36 squares for sashing blocks.

Cut 4 strips each length for inner and outer borders and 4 squares for corners.

5 x 7 Horizontal Setting

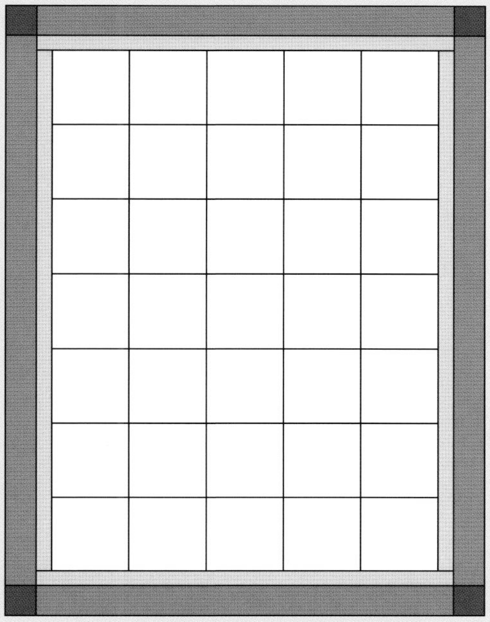

Finished Block	Inner Border	Outer Border	Corner Squares	Finished Size of Quilt
8"	2"	6"	6"	56" x 72"
9"	1½"	4½"	4½"	57" x 75"
10"	2"	5"	5"	64" x 84"
10½"	2"	5"	5"	66½" x 87½"
12"	2"	6"	6"	76" x 100"
14"	3"	6"	6"	88" x 116"

FABRIC REQUIREMENTS (in yards)

Block	Inner Border	Outer Border	Corner Squares	Binding	Backing
8"	½	1⅜	¼	⅔	4⅜
9"	½	1¼	¼	⅔	4¾
10"	⅝	1⅓	¼	¾	5
10½"	⅔	1⅓	¼	¾	5¼
12"	¾	1¾	¼	⅞	5¾
14"	1⅛	2	¼	1	10¼

CUTTING INSTRUCTIONS

Block	Inner Border	Outer Border	Corner Squares	Binding
8"	2½" x 56½"**	6½" x 60½"**	6½"	8
	2½" x 44½"**	6½" x 44½"**		
9"	2" x 63½"**	5" x 66½"**	5"	8
	2" x 48½"**	5" x 48½"**		
10"	2½" x 70½"**	5½" x 74½"**	5½"	9
	2½" x 54½"**	5½" x 54½"**		
10½"	2½" x 74"**	5½" x 78"**	5½"	9
	2½" x 57"**	5½" x 57"**		
12"	2½" x 84½"**	6½" x 88½"**	6½"	10
	2½" x 64½"**	6½" x 64½"**		
14"	3½" x 98½"**	6½" x 104½"**	6½"	12
	3½" x 76½"**	6½" x 76½"**		

** Piece fabric strips to get needed length.
For binding cut the number of 2½" x width of fabric strips listed under binding.

Cut 2 strips each length for inner and outer borders, and 4 squares for corners.

1 x 3 On-Point Setting

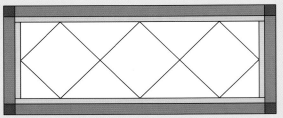

Finished Block	Inner Border	Outer Border	Corner Squares	Finished Size of Quilt
8"	1"	2"	2"	17½" x 40½"
9"	1½"	3"	3"	22" x 48"
10"	2"	3"	3"	24" x 52"
10½"	2"	3"	3"	25" x 55"
12"	2"	4"	4"	29" x 63"
14"	2"	4"	4"	32" x 72"

FABRIC REQUIREMENTS (in yards)

Block	Inner Border	Outer Border	Corner Squares	Setting Triangles	Binding	Backing
8"	¼	⅜	¼	½	⅜	1⅜
9"	¼	½	¼	½	½	1⅔
10"	⅜	½	¼	⅝	½	1¾
10½"	⅜	½	¼	⅝	½	1¾
12"	⅜	¾	¼	⅝	⅝	2
14"	½	1	¼	1	⅝	2⅜

CUTTING INSTRUCTIONS

Block	Inner Border	Outer Border	Corner Squares	Side Triangles	Corner Triangles	Binding
8"	1½" x 12"	2½" x 14"	2½"	12¾"	6⅝"	4
	1½" x 36½"	2½" x 36½"				
9"	2" x 13½"	3½" x 16½"	3½"	14¼"	7⅜"	5
	2" x 42½"**	3½" x 42½"**				
10"	2½" x 14½"	3½" x 18½"	3½"	15¼"	8"	5
	2½" x 46½"**	3½" x 46½"**				
10½"	2½" x 15½"	3½" x 19½"	3½"	16¼"	8½"	5
	2½" x 49½"**	3½" x 49½"**				
12"	2½" x 17½"	4½" x 21½"	4½"	18¼"	9½"	6
	2½" x 55½"**	4½" x 55½"**				
14"	2½" x 20½"	4½" x 24½"	4½"	21¼"	11"	6
	2½" x 64½"**	4½" x 64½"**				

For binding, cut the number of 2½" x width of fabric strips listed under binding.

Cut 2 strips each length for inner and outer borders and 4 squares for corner blocks.

For side setting triangles, cut 1 square and sub-cut into 4 triangles.

For corner setting triangles, cut 2 squares and sub-cut into 2 triangles each.

** Piece fabric strips to get needed length.

2x3 On-Point Setting

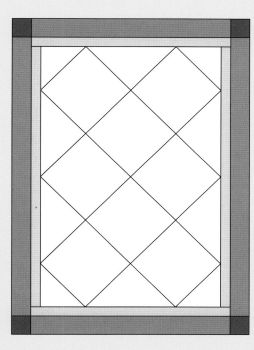

Finished Block	Inner Border	Outer Border	Corner Squares	Finished Size of Quilt
8"	2"	3"	3"	33" x 44"
9"	1½"	3"	3"	35" x 48"
10"	2"	4"	4"	40" x 54"
10½"	2½"	5"	5"	45" x 60"
12"	2"	4"	4"	46" x 63"
14"	2"	4"	4"	52" x 72"

FABRIC REQUIREMENTS (in yards)

Block	Inner Border	Outer Border	Corner Squares	Setting Triangles	Binding	Backing
8"	⅜	½	¼	½	½	1½
9"	⅜	½	¼	¾	½	1¾
10"	½	¾	¼	⅞	⅝	3⅓
10½"	⅝	1	¼	⅞	⅝	3⅝
12"	½	⅞	¼	1	⅝	4
14"	⅝	1	¼	1¼	⅝	5¼

CUTTING INSTRUCTIONS

Block	Inner Border	Outer Border	Corner Squares	Side Triangles	Corner Triangles	Binding
8"	2½" x 35"	3½" x 39"	3½"	12¾"	6⅝"	5
	2½" x 27½"	3½" x 27½"				
9"	2" x 39½"	3½" x 42½"**	3½"	14¼"	7⅜"	5
	2" x 29½"	3½" x 29½"				
10"	2½" x 42½"**	4½" x 46½"**	4½"	15¼"	8"	6
	2½" x 32½"	4½" x 32½"				
10½"	3" x 45½"**	5½" x 50½"**	5½"	16¼"	8½"	6
	3" x 35½"	5½" x 35½"				
12"	2½" x 51½"**	4½" x 55½"**	4½"	18¼"	9½"	7
	2½" x 38½"	4½" x 38½"				
14"	2½" x 60½"**	4½" x 64½"**	4½"	21¼"	11"	7
	2½" x 44½"**	4½" x 44½"**				

For binding, cut the number of 2½" x width of fabric strips listed under binding.

Cut 2 strips each length for inner and outer borders and 4 squares for corner blocks.

For side setting triangles, cut 2 squares and sub-cut into 4 triangles each.

For corner setting triangles, cut 2 squares and sub-cut into 2 triangles each.

** Piece fabric strips to get needed length.

2x4 On-Point Setting

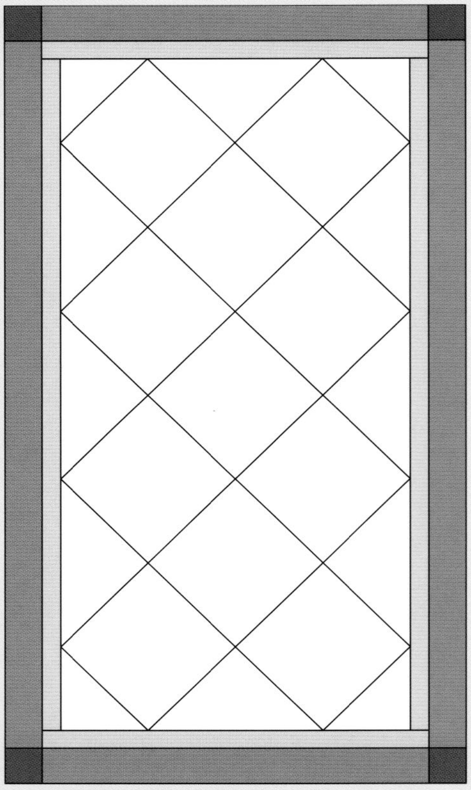

Finished Block	Inner Border	Outer Border	Corner Squares	Finished Size of Quilt
8"	2"	4"	4"	35" x 58"
9"	1½"	3"	3"	35" x 61"
10"	2"	3"	3"	38" x 66"
10½"	2½"	3½"	3½"	42" x 72"
12"	2"	4"	4"	46" x 80"
14"	2"	6"	6"	56" x 96"

FABRIC REQUIREMENTS (in yards)

Block	Inner Border	Outer Border	Corner Squares	Setting Triangles	Binding	Backing
8"	⅜	¾	¼	½	⅝	2
9"	⅜	⅝	¼	¾	⅝	2
10"	½	⅝	¼	⅞	⅝	2⅜
10½"	⅝	⅞	¼	⅞	⅝	4½
12"	⅝	1	¼	1	⅝	5
14"	⅝	1½	¼	1¼	¾	5¾

CUTTING INSTRUCTIONS

Block	Inner Border	Outer Border	Corner Squares	Side Triangles	Corner Triangles	Binding
8"	2½" x 46½"**	4½" x 50½"**	4½"	12¾"	6⅝"	6
	2½" x 27½"	4½" x 27½"				
9"	2" x 52½"**	3½" x 55½"**	3½"	14¼"	7⅜"	6
	2" x 29½"	3½" x 29½"				
10"	2½" x 56½"**	3½" x 60½"**	3½"	15¼"	8"	6
	2½" x 32½"	3½" x 32½"				
10½"	3" x 60½"**	4" x 65½"**	4"	16¼"	8½"	7
	3" x 35½"	4" x 35½"				
12"	2½" x 68½"**	4½" x 72½"**	4½"	18¼"	9½"	7
	2½" x 38½"	4½" x 38½"				
14"	2½" x 80½"**	6½" x 84½"**	6½"	21¼"	11"	9
	2½" x 44½"**	6½" x 44½"				

For binding, cut the number of 2½" x width of fabric strips listed under binding.

Cut 2 strips each length for inner and outer borders and 4 squares for corner squares.

For side setting triangles, cut 2 squares and sub-cut into 4 triangles each.

For corner setting triangles, cut 2 squares and sub-cut into 2 triangles each.

** Piece fabric strips to get needed length.

3x3 On-Point Setting

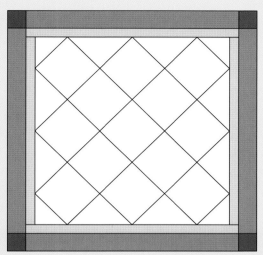

Finished Block	Inner Border	Outer Border	Corner Squares	Finished Size of Quilt
8"	2"	4"	4"	46½" x 46½"
9"	1½"	3"	3"	48" x 48"
10"	2"	4"	4"	54" x 54"
10½"	2½"	5"	5"	60" x 60"
12"	2"	4"	4"	63" x 63"
14"	2"	6"	6"	76" x 76"

FABRIC REQUIREMENTS (in yards)

Block	Inner Border	Outer Border	Corner Squares	Setting Triangles	Binding	Backing
8"	⅜	¾	¼	½	⅝	3
9"	⅜	⅝	¼	¾	⅝	3
10"	½	¾	¼	⅞	⅝	3½
10½"	⅝	1⅛	¼	⅞	⅝	3¾
12"	⅝	1	¼	1	⅝	4
14"	⅝	1½	¼	1¼	¾	4¾

CUTTING INSTRUCTIONS

Block	Inner Border	Outer Border	Corner Squares	Side Triangles	Corner Triangles	Binding
8"	2½" x 35"	4½" x 39"	4½"	12¾"	6⅝"	6
	2½" x 39"					
9"	2" x 39½"	3½" x 42½"**	3½"	14¼"	7⅜"	6
	2" x 42½"**					
10"	2½" x 42½"**	4½" x 46½"**	4½"	15¼"	8"	7
	2½" x 46½"**					
10½"	3" x 45½"**	5½" x 50½"**	5½"	16¼"	8½"	7
	3" x 50½"**					
12"	2½" x 51½"**	4½" x 55½"**	4½"	18¼"	9½"	7
	2½" x 55½"**					
14"	2½" x 60½"**	6½" x 64½"**	6½"	21¼"	11"	9
	2½" x 64½"**					

For binding, cut the number of 2½" x width of fabric strips listed under binding.

Cut 2 strips each length for inner border, 4 strips each length for outer border, and 4 squares for corner squares.

For side setting triangles, cut 2 squares and sub-cut into 4 triangles each.

For corner setting triangles, cut 2 squares and sub-cut into 2 triangles each.

** Piece fabric strips to get needed length.

4 x 4 On-Point Setting

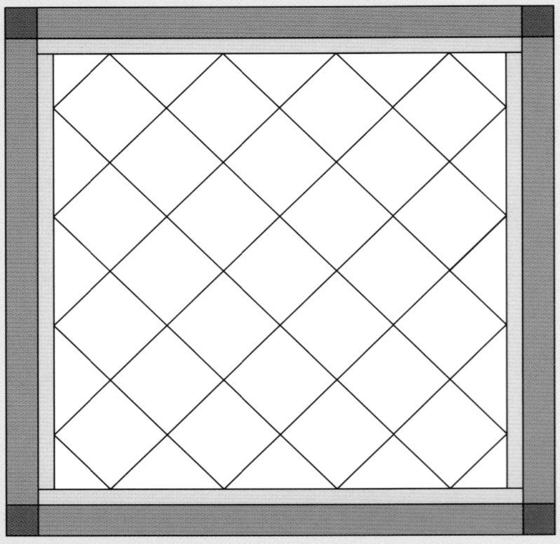

Finished Block	Inner Border	Outer Border	Corner Squares	Finished Size of Quilt
8"	2"	4"	4"	58" x 58"
9"	2"	3"	3"	62" x 62"
10"	2"	5"	5"	70" x 70"
10½"	2½"	5"	5"	75" x 75"
12"	2"	4"	4"	80" x 80"
14"	2"	6"	6"	96" x 96"

FABRIC REQUIREMENTS (in yards)

Block	Inner Border	Outer Border	Corner Squares	Setting Triangles	Binding	Backing
8"	½	⅞	¼	⅔	⅝	3½
9"	⅝	¾	¼	1	⅝	3¾
10"	⅝	1½	¼	1	⅔	4½
10½"	⅞	1½	¼	1¼	¾	4¾
12"	⅔	1¼	¼	1¼	¾	7¼
14"	¾	2	¼	2	⅞	8½

CUTTING INSTRUCTIONS

Block	Inner Border	Outer Border	Corner Squares	Side Triangles	Corner Triangles	Binding
8"	2½" x 46½"**	4½" x 50½"**	4½"	12¾"	6⅝"	7
	2½" x 50½"**					
9"	2½" x 52½"**	3½" x 56½"**	3½"	14¼"	7⅜"	7
	2½" x 56½"**					
10"	2½" x 56½"**	5½" x 60½"**	5½"	15¼"	8"	8
	2½" x 60½"**					
10½"	3" x 60½"**	5½" x 65½"**	5½"	16¼"	8½"	9
	3" x 65½"**					
12"	2½" x 68½"**	4½" x 72½"**	4½"	18¼"	9½"	9
	2½" x 72½"**					
14"	2½" x 80½"**	6½" x 84½"**	6½"	21¼"	11"	11
	2½" x 84½"**					

*** Piece fabric strips to get needed length.*

For binding, cut the number of 2½" x width of fabric strips listed under binding.

Cut 2 strips each length for inner border, 4 strips each for outer border, and 4 squares for corner squares.

For side setting triangles, cut 3 squares and sub-cut into 4 triangles each.

For corner setting triangles, cut 2 squares and sub-cut into 2 triangles each.

4x5 On-Point Setting

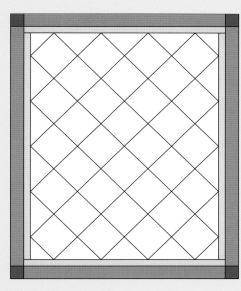

Finished Block	Inner Border	Outer Border	Corner Squares	Finished Size of Quilt
8"	2"	4"	4"	58" x 69½"
9"	2"	4½"	4½"	65" x 78"
10"	2"	5"	5"	70" x 84"
10½"	2½"	5"	5"	75" x 90"
12"	2"	6"	6"	84" x 101"
14"	3"	6"	6"	98" x 118"

FABRIC REQUIREMENTS (in yards)

Block	Inner Border	Outer Border	Corner Squares	Setting Triangles	Binding	Backing
8"	½	1	¼	1	⅔	4¼
9"	⅝	1⅛	¼	1	⅔	4¾
10"	⅝	1⅜	¼	1	¾	5¼
10½"	¾	1½	¼	1⅜	¾	5½
12"	¾	2	¼	1½	⅞	8⅛
14"	1¼	2	¼	2½	1	10⅜

CUTTING INSTRUCTIONS

Block	Inner Border	Outer Border	Corner Squares	Side Triangles	Corner Triangles	Binding
8"	2½" x 58"**	4½" x 62"**	4½"	12¾"	6⅝"	8
	2½" x 50½"**	4½" x 50½"**				
9"	2½" x 65½"**	5" x 69½"**	5"	14¼"	7⅜"	8
	2½" x 56½"**	5" x 56½"**				
10"	2½" x 70½"**	5½" x 74½"**	5½"	15¼"	8"	9
	2½" x 60½"**	5½" x 60½"**				
10½"	3" x 75½"**	5½" x 80½"**	5½"	16¼"	8½"	9
	3" x 65½"**	5½" x 65½"**				
12"	2½" x 85½"**	6½" x 89½"**	6½"	18¼"	9½"	10
	2½" x 72½"**	6½" x 72½"**				
14"	3½" x 100½"**	6½" x 106½"**	6½"	21¼"	11"	12
	3½" x 86½"**	6½" x 86½"**				

For binding, cut the number of 2½" x width of fabric strips listed under binding.

Cut 2 strips each length for inner and outer borders, and 4 squares for corner squares.

For side setting triangles cut 4 squares and sub-cut into 4 triangles each.

For corner setting triangles, cut 2 squares and sub-cut into 2 triangles each.

** *Piece fabric strips to get needed length.*

5x5 On-Point Setting

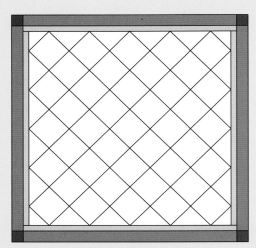

Finished Block	Inner Border	Outer Border	Corner Squares	Finished Size of Quilt
8"	2"	6"	6"	73" x 73"
9"	1½"	4½"	4½"	77" x 77"
10"	1½"	4"	4"	81" x 81"
10½"	1½"	5"	5"	88" x 88"
12"	2"	6"	6"	101" x 101"
14"	2"	6"	6"	116" x 116"

FABRIC REQUIREMENTS (in yards)

Block	Inner Border	Outer Border	Corner Squares	Setting Triangles	Binding	Backing
8"	⅝	1½	¼	1	¾	4½
9"	½	1⅜	¼	1	¾	4¾
10"	⅝	1¼	¼	1	¾	7½
10½"	⅝	1½	¼	1⅜	⅞	7¾
12"	¾	1⅞	¼	1½	⅞	9
14"	⅞	2⅜	¼	2½	1	10½

CUTTING INSTRUCTIONS

Block	Inner Border	Outer Border	Corner Squares	Side Triangles	Corner Triangles	Binding
8"	2½" x 58"**	6½" x 62"**	6½"	12¾"	6⅝"	9
	2½" x 62"**					
9"	2" x 65½"**	5" x 68½"**	5"	14¼"	7⅜"	9
	2" x 68½"**					
10"	2" x 70½"**	4½" x 73½"**	4½"	15¼"	8"	9
	2" x 73½"**					
10½"	2" x 75½"**	5½" x 78½"**	5½"	16¼"	8½"	10
	2" x 78½"**					
12"	2½" x 85½"**	6½" x 89½"**	6½"	18¼"	9½"	11
	2½" x 89½"**					
14"	2½" x 100½"**	6½" x 104½"**	6½"	21¼"	11"	13
	2½" x 104½"**					

For binding, cut the number of 2½" x width of fabric strips listed under binding.

Cut 2 strips each length for inner border, 4 strips each length for outer border, and 4 squares for corner squares.

For side setting triangles, cut 4 squares and sub-cut each into 4 triangles.

For corner setting triangles, cut 2 squares and sub-cut each into 2 triangles.

** Piece fabric strips to get needed length.

Chapter Six

Back-art: "Make Do" Creatively

Some quilters believe that when the top is finished the quilt is done. But even if someone else does the quilting, there is one last decision to make—what to put on the back. The easiest decision is muslin or one of the fabrics used on the front. But, if you buy a length of fabric specifically for the back, there is often a lot of fabric left over.

Now is the time to get creative. "Creative" here is just another way to say, "make something interesting out of leftover units and/or fabrics from the front of the quilt." Each quilt and its circumstances are unique and will speak to you in different ways. Study the following examples, and let them spark creativity in your own quilts.

Expressions of Nature was made for a Moda trunk show, and they sent four different one-yard pieces

Expressions of Nature, back

Small Christmas Star, back

for the back. To add interest, strips left over from the front were joined and randomly inserted in the yard cuts to provide the necessary size and to produce an attractive back.

Once you start thinking creatively about the backs of your quilts, the sky's the limit. Backs can contain block elements from the quilt front or merely the fabrics, as can be seen on *Small Christmas Star* and *Off Center— Out of Control.*

Small Christmas Star starts with a green and cream Nine-Patch from the quilt front. This unit becomes the center of a very large off-center Log Cabin block. Why off-center? Because there was more green fabric left than cream.

The blocks on the front of *Off Center—Out of Control* are 8". The blocks on the back are 16". Exploding the block size for the back gives proportion and punch using only two blocks. Any smaller and the two blocks would look lost. Now the back looks well-proportioned, and well-planned, not just an afterthought.

Off Center—Out of Control, back

On the back of *Black & White and Red All Over* there is one oversized L Block. For balance there is a vertical strip that includes several elements and fabrics from the front. The strip is really just a free-form, design-as-you-go element. Set the elements off-center, both horizontally and vertically, for the best balance.

Depending on how you use your quilt, the back may get a lot of exposure or very little at all. It adds an element of surprise. It's a chance for the normally traditional quilter to try something different. If it doesn't turn out as good as you hoped, you still have a great quilt on the front.

The next time you finish a quilt top, take an afternoon and design an equally interesting back. You may be surprised at what you can create.

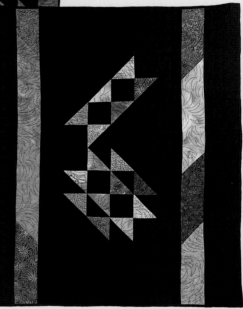

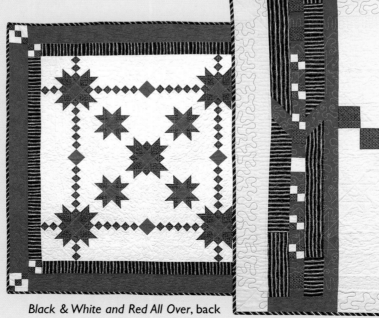

Black & White and Red All Over, back

BIBLIOGRAPHY

Brackman, Barbara, comp. *Encyclopedia of Pieced Quilt Patterns*. Paducah, Kentucky: American Quilter's Society, 1993.

Wolfrom, Joen. *Make Any Block Any Size*. Lafayette, California: C&T Publishing, 1999.

Craig, Sharyn. *Setting Solutions*. Lafayette, California: C&T Publishing, 2001.

RESOURCES

EZ Quilting
85 South Street
West Warren, MA 01092
www.ezquilt.com
(Tri-Recs Tools)

Michell Marketing, Inc.
3525 Broad Street
Chamblee, GA 30341
(Perfect Patchwork Templates)

Electric Quilt Company
419 Gould Street, Suite 2
Bowling Green, OH 43402
www.electricquilt.com
(EQ4 and Block Base)

HQS Inc.
P.O. Box 94237
Phoenix, AZ 85070
(Triangles on a Roll)

Thangles
P.O. Box 2266
Fond du Lac, WI 54936
www.thangles.com
(Thangles)

INDEX